THE POCKET
DARING BOOK FOR GIRLS:
WISDOM AND WONDER

PRAISE FOR *THE DARING BOOK FOR GIRLS*

"An old-fashioned-fun-and survival guide specifically for the pigtail pack . . . offers primers on everything from changing a tire and negotiating pay to basic karate moves and lighthearted pranks. Now Hayley has no excuse for sitting at the computer while Zack is up in his tree house."—*Reader's Digest*

"With tips on doing cartwheels and pulling pranks, *The Daring Book for Girls* is old-school cool—like its bestselling brother *The Dangerous Book for Boys*."—*Good Housekeeping*

"The authors mix inspiring tales of girls who made good . . . with a scrap bag of how-tos for girlish activities . . . *The Daring Book for Girls* keeps . . . practical knowledge from getting drowned in the techno-flow."—*The New York Times*

"The essential how-to manual for the modern-day girl."—*Teen Vogue*

"Not that we're feeling competitive, but *The Dangerous Book for Boys* does seem a wee bit . . . exclusionary. Happily, *The Daring Book for Girls* shows the women of the future—and their adventurous elders (us!)—everything from how to tie a sari to how to negotiate a salary and clues them in on the first rules of softball (never apologize unless you actually bop someone). Among the joys: nearly extinct games (like "Light as a Feather, Stiff as a Board") that may have eluded you while you were busy with Barbie and boy toys."—*O, The Oprah Magazine*

THE POCKET DARING BOOK FOR GIRLS: WISDOM AND WONDER

This book mixes much-loved chapters from the popular *The Daring Book for Girls* with even more stories, facts, and things to know. Great for girls on the go, this portable and pocket-sized book of Wisdom and Wonder is just the thing for anyone who loves to discover new ideas and trade knowledge with family and friends. It's the perfect companion for the adventures that come your way, and for the downtime between them.

Daring Girl badges and other downloads available at
www.daringbookforgirls.com

THE POCKET DARING BOOK FOR GIRLS: WISDOM AND WONDER

For information, address HarperCollins Publishers,
10 East 53rd Street, New York, NY 10022.

HarperCollins books may be purchased for educational, business,
or sales promotional use. For information, please write:
Special Markets Department, HarperCollins Publishers,
10 East 53rd Street, New York, NY 10022.

FIRST EDITION

NOTE TO PARENTS: This book contains a number of activities which may be dangerous if not done exactly as directed or which may be inappropriate for young children. All of these activities should be carried out under adult supervision only. The authors and publishers expressly disclaim liability for any injury or damages that result from engaging in the activities contained in this book.

Illustrations by Alexis Seabrook

Designed by Richard J. Berenson, Berenson Design & Books, LLC and
The Stonesong Press, LLC

Library of Congress Cataloging-in-Publication Data has been applied for.

ISBN: 9-780-061-64994-3

08   09   10   11   12 ❖/QW 10 9 8 7 6 5 4 3 2 1

WISDOM & WONDER

The Pocket

DARING

Book
for

Girls

Andrea J. Buchanan & Miriam Peskowitz

Illustrations by Alexis Seabrook

 **Collins**

An Imprint of HarperCollinsPublishers

Contents

Introduction

We think Wisdom and Wonder is the perfect description for this pocket version of *The Daring Book for Girls*. Within the pages of this portable little book is an impressive amount of things to know and ideas to explore. To build this compendium, we took some of our favorite stories and lore from the original *Daring Book for Girls,* and to those chapters we added even more topics. Alongside queens, pirates, pilots, and spies, we share with you everything from curiosities about tongue twisters and galaxies, to haiku, layers of the earth and air, Doric columns, French Around the World, and the mysterious Fibonacci numbers.

True daring is all about enjoying yourself, exploring new things, and leading an interesting life. We hope this collection spurs you on that journey.

Andrea J. Buchanan
Miriam Peskowitz

Galaxies

Galaxies are enormous, organized systems of stars, star clusters, dust, and gas. As vast as it seems to us here on Earth, our galaxy, the Milky Way, is just one of billions of galaxies in the universe. Exactly how many galaxies exist isn't known—there may be as many as 100 billion galaxies in just the part of the universe scientists can actually observe—and scientists also aren't sure about exactly where galaxies came from and how they were formed. What we do know is that galaxies can contain anywhere from several million to several trillion stars (our own galaxy, the Milky Way, contains somewhere in the neighborhood of 100 billion stars, including the sun); that they can be separated by as little as few thousands of light years to millions of light years in distance; and that they come in three basic shapes: spiral, elliptical, and irregular.

Our galaxy's nickname, the Milky Way, comes from the Greek kyklos *galaktikos,* or "milky circle," which likens its appearance in the distant sky to glistening drops of spilled milk. But why milk? Greek mythology tells the interesting tale. In one of the many colorful stories the

Greeks used to explain the natural world, Zeus (the king of the gods and the god of thunder) tricked Hera (goddess of women and marriage) into breastfeeding his mortal son Heracles by placing the baby on her breast while she was sleeping. His plan was to have the baby drink Hera's milk and thus become a god like him. But Hera awoke and pushed the baby away, causing the milk to spray across the night sky.

SPIRAL

Our Milky Way galaxy is a spiral galaxy, its twisting, whorling shape resembling water circling around a drain, a hurricane as seen from a satellite, or a child's pinwheel blowing in the breeze. Spiral galaxies usually have an "eye" at the center (a disk with a bulging center made up of stars, planets, dust, and gas) and spiraling arms extending outward in a spinning motion. Everything rotates around the galactic center at speeds of hundreds of kilometers per second. A faster or slower rotation can affect a galaxy's shape—such as a kind of spiral galaxy called a "sombrero galaxy," due to its flattened, spread-out appearance. The bulge at the center of the galactic disk is where older stars usually reside, while newer stars

often form in the galaxy's arms. The newer stars are often quite large, and very bright, but they don't last very long: their sheer size causes them to burn out quickly. Smaller stars that aren't quite as luminous last longer.

ELLIPTICAL

Elliptical galaxies often have an elongated, football-like shape. Unlike spiral galaxies they do not have a disk at their center. Elliptical galaxies are also usually smaller than spiral galaxies, and may contain anywhere from a few thousand stars to billions of stars. Most of the stars

in an elliptical galaxies are very old and often clustered together, which makes the center appear as though it is one giant star. It is very rare that new stars form in these types of galaxies. Very large elliptical galaxies, called Giant elliptical galaxies, are the largest galaxies in the universe that we know of, and can be as much as two million light years in length.

IRREGULAR

Irregular galaxies are just what they sound like: irregularly shaped galaxies that are neither spiral nor elliptical. They can appear misshapen or formless. This may be due to repeated collisions with other galaxies, or it may be that they have always been shaped that way.

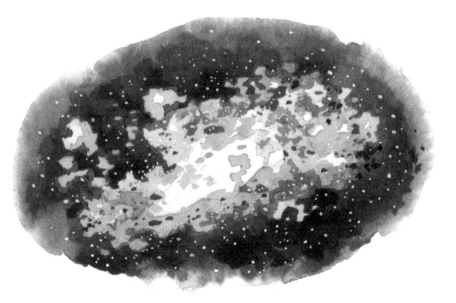

Galactic measurements

The distances between galaxies are so huge, they are usually measured in astronomical units calls megaparsecs. Just one parsec equals about 19,176,075,967,325 miles. A megaparsec is *one million parsecs*—which is about 3.3 million light years. So instead of saying that our nearest neighbor, the Andromeda Galaxy (another spiral system) is 2 to 3 million light years from us, we can say that the distance

between the Milky Way and the Andromeda Galaxy is about 0.899 megaparsecs.

THE MILKY WAY AROUND THE WORLD

In the Baltic languages, the Milky Way is called the "Bird's Path." In ancient China it was called "Heavenly River of Han," and in contemporary China and other parts of Asia it is called "Silver River." In Japan, the

Milky Way is called the "Silver River System" or the "River of Heaven." In Sweden, the Milky Way is called Vintergatan, or "Winter Street."

The term Milky Way first appeared in the English language in 1380 in a poem by Geoffrey Chaucer titled "The House of Fame." (The poem is written in Middle English, which, as you can see in the spelling below, differs from the modern English we use today.)

> *"See yonder, lo, the Galaxy*
> *Which men clepeth the Milky Wey,*
> *For hit is whyt."*

❧

South Sea Islands

The South Sea Islands are rich with history, lore, and fantastical beauty, and are a tropical adventure paradise.

One famous visitor to these remote islands was Pippilotta Delicatessa Windowshade Mackrelmint Efraim's Daughter Longstocking, otherwise known as Pippi, the spunky fictional heroine of the Pippi Longstocking books. In one adventure, red-haired Pippi's pirate father, the swashbuckling Efraim Longstocking, capsizes his boat, The Hoptoad, on a South Sea Isle (the fictional Kurrekurredutt). The locals pronounce him their leader, calling him Fat White Chief. And when Pippi comes to visit with her friends from Sweden, they call her Princess Pippilotta.

Well, that was the 1940s. It has gone out of fashion to barge onto native islands like that, expecting to become the princess and chief, in fiction or in reality. Today, were you to land on a South Sea Island (whether because your own pirate ship takes water in the Pacific, or because the tunnel you were digging from your backyard to China went slightly askew), here are some contemporary and historical details you'll want to know.

FASCINATING FACTS

❧ The South Sea Islands are part of the geographical area called Oceania. This includes more then 10,000 islands in the Pacific Ocean. Some are mere specks of rock in the ocean. Others, like Hawaii, Australia, and New Zealand, are large and well known. The islands are divided into four groups: Australasia, Micronesia, Melanesia, and Polynesia.

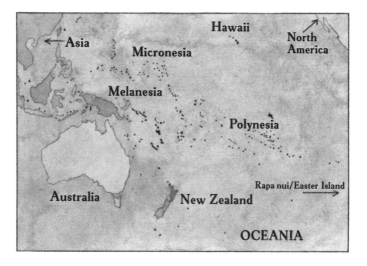

❧ Many of the islands are coral reefs—with villages built on the delicate skeletons of live coral. Some formed from the once-hot lava of underwater volcanoes, which eventually rose to the water's surface.

❧ Additional islands are atolls—that's a narrow circle of land surrounded by ocean, with a lagoon in the middle. Atolls are the result of coral that has grown on top of a volcanic island that over the years and, with changing water levels, has sunk back into the sea. Still others are archipelagos, long chains of islands scattered over an expanse of water.

❧ A good number of the islands are actually territories of far-away nations like the United States, France, and the United Kingdom. A few, like Fiji, the Marshall Islands, Pelau, and Vanuatu, are independent.

CAPTAIN COOK'S VOYAGES TO THE SOUTH SEAS

The famous English explorer Captain James Cook made three voyages through the Pacific islands between 1768 and 1779. Cook was the first European to see Tahiti, to sail around New Zealand, and to set foot in Australia.

A Tahitian man named Omai guided Cook through the islands during his first voyage. Cook brought Omai back to England with him and, on his third and final voyage to the islands, he returned Omai to his home.

Cook left from Tahiti, heading north and then east to the Americas, where he mapped the west coast and tried, unsuccessfully, to find passage back to England through the Bering Strait. He died in Hawaii in 1779.

Tahitian Women on the Beach by Paul Gauguin

PAUL GAUGUIN AND THE SOUTH PACIFIC

Perhaps you have seen French artist Paul Gauguin's vivid paintings of village scenes, huts, and the spiritual life of South Sea Island people, in his trademark oranges and lush greens. Gauguin (1848-1903) embraced these islands. On his last legs as a failed businessman, he left his Danish wife Mette and their five children (forcing them to live with Mette's family to make ends meet) and boarded a ship for the South Pacific. There, he dreamt, he could escape the conventions of European life and the Impressionist school of art, which he found confining.

In Tahiti and the Marquesas Islands, where Gauguin lived the rest of his days, he painted his now renowned images of island life. Gauguin found himself at odds with the European governments established on the islands; it turns out he couldn't really escape Europe after all. The colonial government sentenced him to prison, but he died of illness at the young age of 54, before he could serve his time. Gauguin is buried on the Marquesas Islands, and his work earned fame and fortune only after his death.

WAR BATTLE ON THE SOLOMON ISLANDS

During World War II, the key battle of Guadalcanal took place in the Solomon Islands. The Japanese were using several of the Solomon Islands as bases, hoping to intercept ships between the United States, Australia, and New Zealand. The Allies (the United States and its partners) wanted these islands for their own bases, and to stop Japan's growing control in the South Pacific.

From August 1942 to February 1943, United States

marines and allied forces fought Japanese troops in and near the Solomon Islands. The Allies' victory at Guadalcanal was a major turning point in the war against Japan.

EASTER ISLAND AND THE MOAI STATUES

Deep in the Pacific Ocean sits Rapa Nui, two thousand miles from its nearest neighbors, Tahiti and Chile. Rapa Nui, also known as Easter Island, is famed for its haunting—and huge—human-like stone carvings, the Moai, who stood guard around the whole circle of the island's coast for a thousand years.

The first European to discover Easter Island was the Dutch explorer Admiral Roggeveen, who landed with his caravan of three ships, the *Eagle*, the *Thienhoven*, and the *African Galley* on Easter Day in 1722 (hence the island's English name). They were neither the first nor the last explorers to reach this outpost, as the Polynesians had been there since 400 AD and other Europeans such as Captain Cook were on their way.

Cook visited Rapa Nui/Easter Island in 1774, on the second of his three voyages to the South Sea. He brought along the artist William Hodges, who was trans-

fixed by the Moai statues and made oil paintings of them. A century later, several hundred villagers helped roll two of the Moai statues onto the British ship *HMS Topaze*. The statues were brought back to England and presented to Queen Victoria. The queen made a place for them in the British Museum, where, in Room 24, you can see them today.

In 1888, Chile claimed Easter Island, and transformed it into a giant sheep ranch. The Chilean colonists crowded the native islanders into the small village of Hanga Roa and confined them with a stone wall, even taking some islanders as slaves. Life went from bad to worse. Some natives tried to escape the island in raft-like fishing boats, facing near-certain death on the high seas.

And the remaining statues? In the 1950s Norwegian archaeologists docked at Easter Island, fascinated by reports and pictures of the mysterious Moai. (Once again the history of the South Sea Islands intersects with far-off Scandinavia!) They found the Maoi in sad disrepair. Invaders had taken some, and the rest had been pushed to the ground when missionaries converted the island to Christianity in the 1890s.

Over time, the archaeologists restored nearly 250 of the Maoi statues—some weighing several tons and standing thirty feet tall—hoisting them back onto their ancient stone platforms, each one-half mile from the next, where they circle the mysterious, stark, now treeless island once again, and look out to sea.

EXOTIC NAMES FOR ADVENTUROUS PLACES

The South Sea Islands have amazing native names that paint mental pictures of this faraway world of ethereal beauty: Giao, Hatuti, Rapa Nui, Bora Bora, Makatea, and Tongal; Fanafutti, Olosega, Fatu Hiva, Mangareva, and many more.

Weather Signs and Sayings

Meteorologists use Doppler radar, weather balloons, satellites, and computers to give fairly accurate predictions of what the weather will be like in the near future. But even before we had computerized weather forecasts, we had ways to interpret and predict the weather. Generations ago, people passed down their knowledge about weather signs through rhymes and sayings they taught to their children. As it turns out, those rhyming proverbs based on the observations and wisdom of sailors, farmers, and other outdoorspeople are grounded not only in experience but also in science. So if you're out camping, or hiking, or traveling on foot in nature, far away from technology, you can use some of that lore to determine a fairly reliable reading of the weather. Here are some of the most well known rhymes about weather signs.

"Red sky at night, sailor's delight. Red sky in morning, sailor's warning"

The various colors of the sky are created by rays of sunlight that are split into colors of the spectrum as they bounce off water vapor and dust particles in our atmosphere. When

the atmosphere is filled with lots of dust and moisture, the sunlight coming through it makes the sky appear reddish. This high concentration of particles usually indicates high pressure and stable air coming in from the west, and since weather systems usually move from west to east, that means you'll have good weather for the night. When the sun rises in the eastern sky looking red, that indicates a high water and dust content in the atmosphere, which basically means that a storm system may be moving in your direction. So if you notice a red sky in the morning, pack your umbrella.

"Ring around the moon, rain or snow soon."
You may have noticed some nights it looks like there's a ring around the moon. That halo, which can also form around

the sun, is a layer of cirrus clouds composed of ice crystals that reflect the moon's light like prisms.

This layer of clouds are not rain or snow-producing clouds, but they sometimes show up as a warm front and low pressure area approaches, which can mean inclement weather. The brighter the ring, the greater the chance of rain or snow.

"Clear moon, frost soon."

When the moon sits in a clear, cloudless sky, lore has it that frost is on its way. The weather science behind the saying explains that in a clear atmosphere, with no clouds to keep the heat on earth from radiating into space, a low-temperature night without wind encourages the formation of frost. When clouds cover the sky, they act as a blanket, keeping in the sun's heat absorbed by the earth during the day.

"A year of snow, a year of plenty."

This one seems a bit counter-intuitive, but in fact a season of continuous snow is better for farmland and trees than a season of alternating warm and cold weather. When there's snow throughout the winter, that delays the blossoming of trees until the cold season is fully over. Otherwise, the alternate thawing and freezing that can come with less stable winter weather destroys fruit-bearing trees and winter grains.

"Rainbow in the morning gives you fair warning."

Rainbows always appear in the part of the sky opposite the sun. Most weather systems move from west to east, so a rainbow in the western sky, which would occur in the morning, signifies rain—it's giving you "fair warning" about the rainstorm that may follow. (A rainbow in the eastern sky, conversely, tells you that the rain has already passed.)

The Daring Girls Guide to Danger

Facing your fears can be a rewarding experience, and pushing yourself to new heights will inspire you to face challenges throughout life. Here in no particular order is a checklist of danger and daring. Some you should be able to do right away, but a few you might need to work up to:

1. **Ride a roller coaster.** The biggest roller coaster drops in America include the Kingdom Ka at Six Flags Great Adventure in New Jersey at 418 feet; the Top Thrill Dragster in Ohio at 400 feet; and Superman: The Escape in California at 328 feet.  But the scariest coaster ride in America is still the Cyclone in Coney Island. Built in the 1920s, this comparably small metal and wooden ride packs an unbelievable punch with sudden drops and hairpin turns.

2. **Ride a zip line across the canopy of a rain forest.**
A trip to Costa Rica offers incredible adventures,
including "flying" across the roof of the world 200
feet off the ground with distances between trees of
up to 1,200 feet. Many outdoor centers around the
country also offer zip line courses.

3. **Go white-water rafting.** Most people think looking at
the Grand Canyon from the rim down is scary, but
a true act of daring is to take a white-water rafting
trip down the stretch of Colorado River that cuts
through it. Some trips even include a helicopter
ride for an extra dose of danger!

4. **Have a scary movie festival in your living room.**
Some good ones are *The Exorcist, Jaws, Alien, The
Shining,* and Alfred Hitchcock's classic but still
frightening *Psycho.* But don't blame us if you can't
go sleep without wondering what's under the bed.

5. **Wear high heels.** This may not sound so dangerous,
but without practice you can fall or twist an ankle.
For your first time in heels, borrow someone else's,

and make sure to start on a hard surface like wood. Once you're feeling steady on your feet, give carpeting a try. If you can wear heels on a thick carpet, you can do anything. Eventually, if it's a skill you want to learn, you'll be able to run, jump, and do karate in three-inch heels.

6. **Stand up for yourself—or someone else.** It's scary to feel like you're the only one who doesn't agree, but when something's wrong, a daring girl speaks up, for herself or someone who needs an ally. Summon your courage and raise your voice—real bravery is feeling the fear and doing it anyway.

7. **Try sushi or another exotic food.** California rolls do not count. For the true daring girl try some *natto* (fermented soy beans) or *escargot* (snails).

8. **Dye your hair purple.** Sometimes the scariest thing is just being a little bit different, even for a day. There are many hair dyes that wash out after a few weeks—so you can experience what it would be like to have a lime-green ponytail without having to wait for all your hair to grow out to change it again.

Elements and Atoms

♦ Elements are basic pieces of matter, composed of a single unique kind of atom. There is nothing that's not made of elements. We know of 111 natural elements, and 7 that have been made only in the laboratory. Some elements—like silver, gold, tin, sulfur, copper and arsenic—were known in classical antiquity, and native peoples of the Americas knew about platinum. Others were discovered during Europe's Age of Science, and more recently.

♦ Four elements were discovered by female scientists.

Element	Abbreviation/ Atomic Number	Discovered By	Date
Polonium	Po/84	Marie Sklodowska Curie	1898
Radium	Ra/88	Marie Sklodowska Curie with her husband Pierre Curie	1898
Rhenium	Re/75	Ida Tacke-Noddack with her colleagues Walter Noddack and Otto Carl Berg	1925
Francium	Fr/87	Marguerite Catherine Perey	1939

♦ An atom is the basic building block of everything. A group of atoms is called a molecule, and molecules form everything we know, live in, and touch.

♦ Inside an atom are protons, neutrons, electrons, quarks and gluons, none of which are visible to our eyes, unfortunately.

♦ Protons are found in the atom's nucleus and carry a positive charge. Each element has a unique number of protons, and the number of protons in an atom never changes. Hydrogen, H, always has 1 proton; Aluminum, Al, always has 13. The proton number distinguishes one element from the others, and accounts for each elements character and behavior. The number of protons determines the order of elements on the Periodic Table. Os, or Osmium, is not the random 76th element, it has 76 protons, and hence its place on the chart.

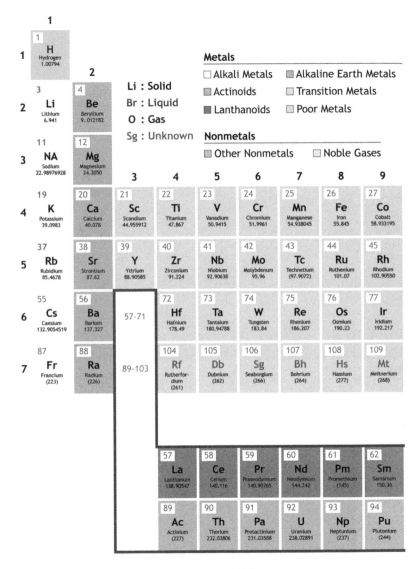

Periodic Table of Elements

			13	**14**	**15**	**16**	**17**	**18**
								2 **He** Helium 4.002603
			5 **B** Boron 10.811	6 **C** Carbon 12.0107	7 **N** Nitrogen 14.0067	8 **O** Oxygen 15.9994	9 **F** Fluorine 18.9984032	10 **Ne** Neon 20.1797
10	**11**	**12**	13 **Al** Aluminium 26.9815386	14 **Si** Silicon 28.0855	15 **P** Phosphorus 30.973762	16 **S** Sulfur 32.065	17 **Cl** Chlorine 35.453	18 **Ar** Argon 39.948
28 **Ni** Nickel 58.6934	29 **Cu** Copper 63.546	30 **Zn** Zinc 65.38	31 **Ga** Gallium 69.723	32 **Ge** Germanium 72.64	33 **As** Arsenic 74.92160	34 **Se** Selenium 78.96	35 **Br** Bromine 79.904	36 **Kr** Krypton 83.798
46 **Pd** Palladium 106.42	47 **Ag** Silver 107.8682	48 **Cd** Cadmium 112.411	49 **In** Indium 114.818	50 **Sn** Tin 118.710	51 **Sb** Antimony 121.760	52 **Te** Tellurium 127.60	53 **I** Iodine 126.90447	54 **Xe** Xenon 131.293
78 **Pt** Platinum 195.084	79 **Au** Gold 196.966569	80 **Hg** Mercury 200.59	81 **Tl** Thallium 204.3833	82 **Pb** Lead 207.2	83 **Bi** Bismuth 208.98040	84 **Po** Polonium (208.9824)	85 **At** Astatine (209.9871)	86 **Rn** Radon (222.0176)
110 **Ds** Darmstadtium (271)	111 **Rg** Roentgenium (272)	112 **Uub** Ununtrium (285)	113 **Uut** Ununtrium (284)	114 **Uuq** Ununquadium (289)	115 **Uup** Ununpentium (288)	116 **Uuh** Ununhexium (292)	117 **Uus** Ununseptium	118 **Uuo** Ununoctium (294)

63 **Eu** Europium 151.25	64 **Gd** Gadolinium 157.25	65 **Tb** Terbium 158.92535	66 **Dy** Dysprosium 162.500	67 **Ho** Holmium 164.93032	68 **Er** Erbium 167.259	69 **Tm** Thulium 168.93421	70 **Yb** Ytterbium 173.054	71 **Lu** Lutetium 174.9668
95 **Am** Americum (243)	96 **Cm** Curium (247)	97 **Bk** Berkelium (247)	98 **Cf** Californium (251)	99 **Es** Einsteinium (252)	100 **Fm** Fermium (257)	101 **Md** Mendelevium (258)	102 **No** Nobelium (259)	103 **Lr** Lawrencium (262)

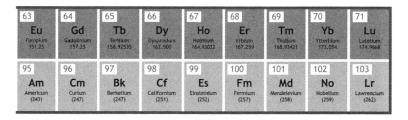

ELEMENTS AND ATOMS

- Neutrons are in the nucleus, and carry a neutral charge.

- Both protons and neutrons break down into quarks, and quarks are held together by gluons.

- Electrons have a negative electrical charge and they orbit around the nucleus. The sharing of electrons between atoms creates bonds. In metals, the movement of electrons between atoms can generate electrical current.

Queens of the Ancient World: Wise Artemisia

It is a mystery what Queen Artemisia, who lived during the fifth century BC, looked like; no depictions of her survive. But the tales we know of her from the world's first historian, Herodotus, portray Artemisia as an intelligent and clever queen who bravely spoke her mind, even when no one else agreed with her. We also know she was a skillful and courageous sailor, who protected the Persian fleet during the ancient Greco-Persian Wars.

In the fifth century BC, Artemisia ruled Halicarnassus (today called Bodrum), a city nestled along a cove on the southeastern coast of Turkey's Aegean Sea. Artemisia's father and her husband had ruled the city before her. When her husband died, she became queen, as their son was too young to rule.

At this time, in 480 BC, the Persian Empire was at its zenith. Xerxes (pronounced *Zerk-si*), the fourth of the great Persian kings, was in power. He had already conquered much of Asia and turned his sights toward the Greek city states and isles.

Xerxes narrowly won the battle of Thermopylae, capturing the pass to the Greek mainland, and then burned down its capital, Athens. He next headed south to take the island of Salamis, moving his battle to sea and relying heavily on the boats in his navy. He asked his allies around the Aegean Sea to send reinforcements. Loyal to Persia, Artemisia loaned five ships to Xerxes' war effort, large triremes, each with a grand sail, and powered by men from Halicarnassus rowing long oars out the sides. She herself took command.

Yet Artemisia was different from many ancient queens (and kings), whom we are told wanted only to battle. When Xerxes asked his general Mardonius to gather the commanders for counsel before storming Salamis, they all encouraged him to go ahead with the sea battle and assured him of victory. Except Artemisia. She warned Xerxes that the Greek ships were stronger than their own. She reminded him that he already held Greece's mainland with Athens and had lost many troops at Thermopylae. She contradicted all the other commanders in advising him to quit while he was ahead.

Xerxes admired Artemisia, but he decided, fatefully, to go with the opinion of the majority. The battle went

wrong—terribly wrong—as Artemisia had predicted. Battle's end found the Persians watching from shore as their ships burned. Still, Artemisia kept her word to Xerxes and commanded her ship. She came under pursuit by an Athenian ship and faced a terrible decision either to be captured or to run into the Persian ships that were ahead of her.

Artemisia made the decision to save her crew, ramming one her allies' ships and sinking it in the effort to escape from the Greek ship. Some have said that she had a longstanding grudge against its commander, King Dam-asithymos of Calyndia. The commander of the Greek vessel chasing her turned away, assuming perhaps she was a sister Greek ship, or even a deserter from the Persian navy. The Persians lost the battle at Salamis, all the men on the Calyndian ship died, but Artemisia and her crew escaped unharmed.

After that battle, Herodotus tells us, King Xerxes again sought advice from his commanders. And again all the commanders wanted to stay and fight for the Grecian islands, except Artemisia. Disagreeing with the group once more, the level-headed queen counseled Xerxes to consider another option: leave 300,000 soldiers behind to hold the mainland and return to Persia himself with the rest of his navy.

Artemisia reminded Xerxes for a second time that he had already torched Athens and taken the Greek city-states. It was enough. The king took Artemisia's wisdom more seriously this time, knowing she had been right before. This time, he listened to the wise woman over the majority, choosing to leave a contingent of troops in Greece and turn toward home instead of battling.

And after that? Herodotus makes a brief mention of

Artemisia ushering Xerxes' sons from Greece to safety in the city of Ephesus, on the Turkish mainland. After that, we have no further information about Artemisia's life. Herodotus concerns himself with describing the next battle, and the next, and because Artemisia declines to fight, she disappears from his pages.

A small vase provides our last evidence of Artemisia: a white jar, made of calcite, that is now at the British Museum. Xerxes gave the jar to Artemisia, a gift for her loyalty and service, and he inscribed it with his royal signature. Artemesia must have bequeathed the jar to her son, and from there, it stayed a family treasure for generations. One hundred years later, another member of her royal line, also named Artemisia, built a burial monument to her husband—the Mausoleum of Halicarnassus, one of the Seven Wonders of the Ancient World. There, in the 1850s, the British archaeologist Charles Newton excavated Xerxes' gift to the first Artemisia and uncovered the final trace of the wise queen.

~

Pirate Stories

There have been women pirates throughout the ages, from Queen Artemisia to female Vikings to modern-day women pirates in the Philippines. Many of the stories about female pirates are just that: made-up stories showcasing women pirates who are merely fictional. But there are several women pirates whose stories are verifiable, and who really did live and (in some cases) die a pirate's life on the high seas.

CHARLOTTE BADGER

Charlotte Badger was a convicted felon when she was sent to Australia from England. She was found guilty of the crime of breaking and entering when she was eighteen years old and sentenced to seven years deportation. She sailed to Port Jackson, Sydney, aboard the convict ship *The Earl of Cornwallis* in 1801 and served five years of her sentence at a factory, during which time she also gave birth to a daughter.

With just two years of her sentence left, she was assigned to work as a servant to a settler in Hobart Town, Tasmania, along with fellow prisoner Catherine Hagerty. In April 1806, Charlotte, her daughter, Catherine, and several male convicts traveled to Hobart Town on a ship called *Venus*. When the *Venus* docked at Port Dalrymple in June, the convicts mutinied, and Charlotte and her friend Catherine joined in with the male convicts to seize control of the ship. The pirate crew headed for New Zealand (even though nobody aboard really knew how to navigate the ship), and Charlotte, her child, Catherine, and two of the male convicts were dropped off at Rangihoua Bay in the Bay of Islands.

Charlotte and her compatriots built huts and lived on the shore of the island, but by 1807, Catherine Hagerty was dead, and the two men had fled. The *Venus* had long since been overtaken by South Sea islanders, who captured the crew and then burned the ship. Charlotte and her child stayed on Rangihoua Bay, living alongside the Maori islanders. Twice she was offered passage back to Port Jackson, and twice she refused, saying that she preferred to die among the Maori.

What happened to Charlotte after 1807 isn't entirely clear. Some stories have her living with a Maori chieftain and bearing another child; in other stories the Maori turned on her, prompting her and her daughter to flee to Tonga; still other stories eventually place her in America, having stowed away on another ship. Whatever happened to her, she was quite possibly the first European woman to have lived in New Zealand, and one of New Zealand's first women pirates.

ANNE BONNY AND MARY READ

Anne Bonny, born in Ireland around 1700, is by all accounts one of the best known female pirates. She was disowned by her father when, as a young teen, she married a sailor named James Bonny; the newlyweds then left Ireland for the Bahamas. There, James worked as an informant, turning in pirates to the authorities for a tidy sum. While James confronted pirates, Anne befriended them: she became especially close with Jack Rackam, also known as "Calico Jack." Jack was a pirate who had sworn off pirating so as to receive amnesty from the Bahamian governor, who had promised not to prosecute any pirate who gave up his pirating ways. In 1719, however, Anne and Jack ran off together, and Jack promptly returned to pirating—this time with Anne by his side. She donned men's clothing in order to join the crew on his ship, the *Revenge,* and was so good at the work that she was accepted as a crewmate even by those men who discovered she was actually a woman.

When the *Revenge* took another ship during a raid and absorbed its crew, Anne discovered she was no longer the only woman on board: a woman by the name of Mary Read had also disguised herself as a man to be accepted as a pirate. Mary, born in London in the late 1600s, had spent nearly her whole life disguised as a man. Mary's mother had raised her as a boy almost from birth to keep the family out of poverty. (Mary's father died before she was born, and her brother, who would have been the only legal heir, also died. Back then, only men could inherit wealth, so baby Mary became baby Mark.) As a young girl living as a boy, Mary worked as a messenger and eventually enlisted in the infantry, fighting in Flanders and serving with distinction. She fell in love with another soldier (to whom she revealed her true gender), and they soon married, leaving the army to run a tavern called The Three Horseshoes. Sadly, her husband died

PIRATE STORIES

in 1717, and Mary once again had to disguise herself as a man to earn a living. She put on her dead husband's clothes, enlisted in the army, and went to Holland. She found no adventure there, so she boarded a ship for the West Indies. That was when her ship was captured by the *Revenge,* and her life intersected with those of Calico Jack and his mistress, Anne Bonny.

Anne and Mary became close friends, and once Anne knew the truth about Mary, she swore that she would never reveal Mary's true identity. But Calico Jack, jealous of Anne's attention, grew suspicious of their friendship and demanded an explanation. Soon the secret was out, but, luckily for Mary, Jack was relieved and not angered to discover she was a woman. He allowed her to continue on the crew, and just as Anne had been accepted by her crewmates despite being female, Mary was accepted too. Unfortunately for the crew of the *Revenge,* the Bahamian governor was not so accepting of pirates who flouted amnesty agreements by returning to pirating after promising not to, and he issued a proclamation naming Jack Rackam, Anne Bonny, and Mary Read as "Pirates and Enemies to the Crown of Great Britain."

In 1720, the *Revenge* was attacked by a pirate-hunter

eager to capture an enemy of the Crown. Calico Jack, along with nearly the entire crew, was drunk at the time, and the men quickly retreated to hide below deck and wait out the attack. Only Anne and Mary stayed above, fighting for the ship. It is said that Anne shouted to the crew, "If there's a man among ye, ye'll come out and fight like the men ye are thought to be!" Enraged by the crew's cowardice, Anne and Mary shot at them, killing one man and wounding several others, including Calico Jack. Despite the women's efforts, the ship was captured.

The crew was taken to Jamaica and tried for piracy in November of 1720. All of them were hanged, save for Anne and Mary, who were granted stays of execution due to the fact that they were both pregnant. Mary was brave in the face of her punishment, telling the court, "As to hanging, it is no great hardship. For were it not for that, every cowardly fellow would turn pirate and so unfit the sea, that men of courage must starve." But as it turned out, Mary never had to face the gallows: she died in prison of a fever. As for Anne, after the piracy trial, the historical record is silent. Rumors say alternately that she was hanged a year later; that she was given a reprieve; that she reconciled with the father who disowned her, or with her first husband, whom she had left; that she gave up the pirate's life and became instead a nun. We may never know for sure what happened to her.

CHING SHIH

Ching Shih—also known as Shi Xainggu, Cheng I Sao, Ching Yih Saou, or Zheng Yi Sao—ruled the South China Sea in the early 19th century, overseeing about 1,800 ships and 80,000 male and female pirates.

She became the commander of the infamous Red Flag Fleet of pirates after her husband Cheng Yi, the former commander from a long line of pirates, died in 1807; she went on to marry Chang Pao, formerly her husband's right-hand man. To say that Ching Shih ran a tight ship was an understatement: pirates who committed even innocuous offenses were beheaded. Her attitude in battle was even more intense, with hundreds of ships and thousands of pirates used to engage even a small target.

Ching Shih was also a ruthless businesswoman. She handled all business matters herself, and pirates not only needed her approval to embark on a raid, they were also required to surrender the entire haul to her. She diversified her business plan by expanding beyond the raiding

of commercial ships, working with shadowy business-
men in the Guangdong salt trade to extort the local salt
merchants. Every ship passing through her waters had to
buy protection from her, and Ching Shih's fleet of mercenaries torched any vessel that refused to pay up.

The Red Flag Fleet under Ching Shih's rule could not
be defeated—not by Chinese officials, not by the Portuguese navy, not by the British. But in 1810, amnesty
was offered to all pirates, and Ching Shih took advantage
of it, negotiating pardons for nearly all her troops. She
retired with all her ill-gotten gains and ran a gambling
house until her death in 1844.

RACHEL WALL

Rachel Schmidt was born in Carlisle, Pennsylvania, in
1760. When she was sixteen, she met George Wall, a
former privateer who served in the Revolutionary War;
against the wishes of her mother, she married him. The
two moved to Boston, where George worked as a fisherman and Rachel worked as a maid in Beacon Hill.
George, whom Rachel's mother had considered more
than slightly shady to begin with, fell in with a rough
crowd and gambled away what money they had. Unable

to pay the rent, and lured by the fun of his fast-living fisherman friends, he hit upon pirating as the answer to their financial woes and convinced Rachel to join in.

George and Rachel stole a ship at Essex and began working as pirates off the Isle of Shoals. They would trick the passing ships by having the blue-eyed, brown-haired Rachel pose as a damsel in distress, standing at the ship's mast and screaming for help as passing ships floated by. Once the rescuing crew came aboard to help, George and his men would kill them, steal their booty, and sink their ship. Rachel and George were successful as pirates, capturing a dozen boats, murdering two dozen sailors, and stealing thousands of dollars in cash and valuables.

Their evil plan was cut short in 1782, when George, along with the rest of his crew, was drowned in a storm. Rachel, who really did need rescuing in that situation, was saved, brought ashore, and taken back to Boston, but it was hard to leave her pirating ways. She spent her days working as a maid, but by night she broke into the cabins of ships docked in Boston Harbor, stealing any goods she could get her hands on.

Her luck ran out in 1789, when she was accused of robbery. At her trial, she admitted to being a pirate but refused to confess to being a murderess or a thief. She was convicted and sentenced to death by hanging. She died on October 8, 1789, the first and possibly the only woman pirate in all of New England, and the last woman to be hanged in Massachusetts.

࿐

States, Statehood, Capitals, Flowers, and Trees— Plus Canada!

★ The original 13 colonies were Connecticut, Delaware, Georgia, Maryland, Massachusetts, New Hampshire, New Jersey, New York, North Carolina, Pennsylvania, Rhode Island, South Carolina, Virginia. They became states in 1776.

★ The fourteenth state was Vermont, in 1791.

★ The Confederate States in the American Civil War were South Carolina, Mississippi, Florida, Alabama, Georgia, Louisiana, Texas, Arkansas, North Carolina, and Tennessee.

★ On the Union Side during the Civil War were the following states: California, Connecticut, Delaware, Illinois, Indiana, Iowa, Kansas, Kentucky, Maine, Maryland, Massachusetts, Michigan, Minnesota, Missouri, Nevada, New Hampshire, New Jersey,

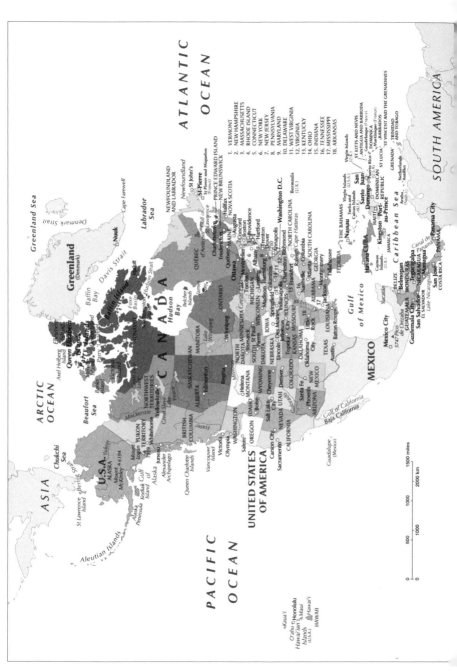

New York, Ohio, Oregon, Pennsylvania, Rhode Island, Vermont, West Virginia, and Wisconsin. (Kentucky and Missouri did not secede, but a rival government, or "rump group," proclaimed secession within both of these states.)

★ The 49th and 50th states were Alaska, in January 1959; and Hawaii, in August 1959.

★ The national bird is the Bald Eagle, the national plant is the rose (made official on October 7, 1986), and the national tree is the oak.

★ A state can change its state tree, as Kentucky did in 1976 when it changed its tree from the tulip poplar (*Liriodendron tulipifera*) to Kentucky coffee tree (*Gymnocladus dioica*). The tree was changed back in 1994, thanks to avid supporters of the tulip poplar. (But don't fret: the Kentucky coffee tree got the title of "State Heritage Tree" out of the deal.)

★ The most popular state tree is the sugar maple (Acer saccharum), which is the state tree for New York, West Virginia, Wisconsin, and Vermont.

★ Washington, D.C., is the capital of the United States, but it is not a state itself. Situated between Maryland and Virginia, it was founded on July 16, 1790, and was developed from its inception as the permanent national headquarters for our government. Article One of our Constitution grants the United States Congress supreme authority over the District, which has one at-large Congressional delegate (who is not allowed to vote in Congress) and no senators.

᧞

State	Date of statehood	Capital	State Flower	State Tree
Alabama	1819	Montgomery	Camellia	Longleaf Pine
Alaska	1959	Juneau	Forget-Me-Not	Sitka Spruce
Arizona	1912	Phoenix	Saguaro Cactus Blossom	Palo verde
Arkansas	1836	Little Rock	Apple Blossom	Loblolly Pine
California	1850	Sacramento	California Poppy	California Redwoods
Colorado	1876	Denver	Rocky Mountain Columbine	Colorado Blue Spruce
Connecticut	1776	Hartford	Mountain Laurel	Charter White Oak
Delaware	1776	Dover	Peach Blossom	American Holly
Florida	1845	Tallahassee	Orange Blossom	Sabal Palmetto
Georgia	1776	Atlanta	Cherokee Rose	Live Oak
Hawaii	1959	Honolulu	Hawaiian Hibiscus (ma'o hau hele)	Kukui Nut Tree
Idaho	1890	Boise	Mock Orange	Western White Pine
Illinois	1818	Springfield	Violet	White Oak
Indiana	1816	Indianapolis	Peony	Tulip-tree
Iowa	1846	Des Moines	Wild Prairie Rose	Oak
Kansas	1861	Topeka	Sunflower	Cottonwood

State	Date of statehood	Capital	State Flower	State Tree
Kentucky	1792	Frankfort	Goldenrod	Tulip Poplar
Louisiana	1812	Baton Rouge	Magnolia	Bald Cypress
Maine	1820	Augusta	White Pine Cone and Tassel	Eastern White Pine
Maryland	1776	Annapolis	Black-Eyed Susan	White Oak
Massachusetts	1776	Boston	Mayflower	American Elm
Michigan	1837	Lansing	Apple Blossom	Eastern White Pine
Minnesota	1858	Saint Paul	Pink and White Lady's Slipper	Red Pine
Mississippi	1817	Jackson	Magnolia	Magnolia
Missouri	1821	Jefferson City	White Hawthorn Blossom	Flowering Dogwood
Montana	1889	Helena	Bitterroot	Ponderosa Pine
Nebraska	1867	Lincoln	Goldenrod	Cottonwood
Nevada	1864	Carson City	Sagebrush	Single-Leaf Pinyon
New Hampshire	1776	Concord	Purple Lilac	American White Birch
New Jersey	1776	Trenton	Violet	Northern Red Oak
New Mexico	1912	Santa Fe	Yucca Flower	Pinyon
New York	1776	Albany	Rose	Sugar Maple

State	Date of statehood	Capital	State Flower	State Tree
North Carolina	1776	Raleigh	American Dogwood	Longleaf Pine
North Dakota	1889	Bismarck	Wild Prairie Rose	American Elm
Ohio	1803	Columbus	Scarlet Carnation	Ohio Buckeye
Oklahoma	1907	Oklahoma City	Oklahoma Rose	Eastern Redbud
Oregon	1859	Salem	Oregon Grape	Douglas Fir
Pennsylvania	1776	Harrisburg	Mountain Laurel	Eastern Hemlock
Rhode Island	1776	Providence	Violet	Red Maple
South Carolina	1776	Columbia	Yellow Jessamine	Cabbage Palmetto
South Dakota	1889	Pierre	Pasque Flower	Black Hills Spruce
Tennessee	1796	Nashville	Iris	Tulip Poplar
Texas	1845	Austin	Bluebonnet	Pecan
Utah	1896	Salt Lake City	Sego Lily	Blue Spruce
Vermont	1791	Montpelier	Red Clover	Sugar Maple
Virginia	1776	Richmond	American Dogwood	Flowering Dogwood
Washington	1889	Olympia	Coast Rhododendron	Western Hemlock
West Virginia	1863	Charleston	Rhododendron	Sugar Maple

State	Date of statehood	Capital	State Flower	State Tree
Wisconsin	1848	Madison	Wood Violet	Sugar Maple
Wyoming	1890	Cheyenne	Indian Paintbrush	Plains Cottonwood

SEVEN THINGS YOU PROBABLY DIDN'T KNOW ABOUT CANADA

1. A Canadian invented basketball. (James Naismith, a physical education instructor from Almonte, Ontario, came up with the game in 1891 while working at the YMCA International Training School in Springfield, Massachusetts.)

2. Parts of Canada are located further to the south than parts of the US. (Toronto is further south than much of New England and the northern Midwest.)

3. Canadians celebrate Thanksgiving on the second Monday in October, not in November.

4. Canadians do not have $1 and $2 bills. Instead, they use coins, known unabashedly as Loonies ($1) and Toonies ($2).

5. America actually invaded Canada twice, in 1775 and 1812, and was rebuffed both times.

6. Canada has 10 provinces and three territories. The provinces are Alberta, British Columbia, Manitoba, New Brunswick, Newfoundland and Labrador, Nova Scotia, Ontario, Prince Edward Island, Quebec, and Saskatchewan. The three territories are the Northwest Territories, Nunavut, and Yukon. Nunavut was the last territory to be added, in 1999.

7. The languages most spoken in Canada are English, French, and Chinese. New Brunswick is the only officially bilingual province (English and French), and in Quebec, French is the official governmental language.

Tongue Twisters

How much wood would a woodchuck chuck if a wood-chuck could chuck wood?

Lots of kids have spent recess rolling their tongues around this and other tongue twisters, but just how does a tongue twister work? In English sentences, similar sounds are usually separated so they are easier to say. Tongue twisters break this rule. They are filled to the brink with phonemes, which are sounds that differ only slightly from each other, like *skunk* and *thunk* and *stunk,* or *mixed* and *biscuits.* Tongue twisters are also filled with alliteration, which means that many of the words start with the same sound, as in *Sure the ship's shipshape, sir.* Because we don't usually say these sounds so quickly and close together, our brains get stumped and our tongues twisted.

Tongue twisters have long been used to teach proper and precise pronunciation to schoolchildren, since only with the clearest articulation might one stand a chance of saying these without a mumble. That makes them especially useful to twirl around your tongue to prepare for a play, a speech, or any time you need to enunciate your syllables and separate your p's from your b's. People learning English for the first time have been known to practice tongue twisters to learn sounds.

Every language has tongue twisters. From the Wolof language of Senegal comes *Tuki fuki buki gudi. Tuki fuki buki becheck,* which means, "Traveling hyenas during the night, traveling hyenas during the day". From Swedish comes *Barbros bror badade bara i Barsebäck,* which means "Barbra's brother only bathes in Barsebäck" (a city in the south of Sweden).

Try saying these tongue twisters fives times fast, or ten:

Is this your sister's sixth zither, sir?

Girl gargoyle, guy gargoyle.

The myth of Miss Muffet.

A whirling roaring rhythmic waltz.

She sold six Swiss wristwatches.

**Classic Two-word
Tongue Twisters**
Inchworms itching.
Unique New York.
Irish Wristwatch.
Selfish shellfish.

Cows graze in groves on grass which grows
in grooves in groves.

On mules we find two legs behind
and two we find before.
We stand behind before we find
what those behind be for.

A skunk sat on a stump
and thunk the stump
stunk, but the stump
thunk the skunk stunk.

Gertie's great-grandma grew aghast at
Gertie's grammar.

Peter Piper picked a peck of pickled
peppers. Did Peter Piper pick a peck
of pickled peppers? If Peter Piper
picked a peck of pickled peppers,
where's the peck of pickled peppers
Peter Piper picked?

Betty Botter bought some butter,
"But," she said, "this butter's bitter.
If I bake this bitter butter,
It will make my batter bitter.
But a bit of better butter—
That would make my batter better."
So she bought a bit of butter,
Better than her bitter butter,
And she baked it in her batter,
And the batter was not bitter.
So 'twas better Betty Botter
Bought a bit of better butter.

Pilots

AMELIA EARHART

Amelia Mary Earhart, born in 1897, was a pilot who received the Distinguished Flying Cross—and worldwide fame—for being the first woman to fly solo across the Atlantic Ocean. She was twenty-one when she saw her first flying exhibition in 1918, and she was captivated. An aircraft flew low to buzz the crowd, and Amelia later said of the experience, "I did not understand it at the time, but I believe that little red airplane said something to me as it swished by." The next year, she began flying lessons with female aviator Anita "Neta" Snook. After six months of lessons, she bought a used yellow biplane that she nicknamed "The Canary," and in October 1922 she flew it to an altitude of 14,000 feet, setting a world record for women pilots. In May 1923, she became the sixteenth

Amelia Earhart

woman to be issued a pilot's license by the Fédération Aéronautique Internationale (FAI). She not only broke aviation records, she also formed a women's flying organization (The Ninety-Nines) and wrote best-selling books. She was the first woman to fly across the Atlantic, the first woman to fly across the Atlantic alone, and the first person, man or woman, to fly across the Atlantic alone twice. She was the first person to fly solo across the Pacific between Honolulu and Oakland, California; the first person to fly solo nonstop from Mexico City to Newark, New Jersey; and the first woman to fly nonstop coast-to-coast across the United States. Her final accomplishment was becoming an enduring mystery: at age thirty-nine, in 1937, Amelia disappeared over the Pacific Ocean during an attempt at making a circumnavigational flight. The official search efforts lasted nine days, but Amelia Earhart was never found.

BESSIE COLEMAN

In 1921, Bessie Coleman, known as "Queen Bess," became the first American (man or woman) to earn an international pilot's license, and the first black woman to earn an aviator's license. One of thirteen children,

Coleman discovered airplanes after graduating from high school, but she couldn't find an aviation school that would teach a black woman to fly. She went to Paris, where she was able to train and earn her license. She became an exhibition flyer, performing daredevil stunts like loop-de-loops and figure eights at airshows across the country, where she was often billed as "the world's greatest woman flyer." She died in 1926, at the age of 34. She was inducted into the Women in Aviation Hall of Fame posthumously, in 1995.

JACQUELINE COCHRAN

Jacqueline Cochran, who in 1953 became the first woman to break the sound barrier, holds more distance and speed records than any pilot, male or female. She was the first woman to take off from and land on an aircraft carrier; to reach Mach 2; to fly a fixed-wing jet aircraft across the Atlantic; to enter the Bendix Trans-continental Race; and to pilot a bomber across the north Atlantic. She was the first pilot to make a blind landing, the first woman in Ohio's Aviation Hall of Fame, and the only woman to ever be president of the Fédération Aéronautique Internationale.

∂

Haiku

Haiku is a Japanese form of poetry. In English, a haiku consists of three lines: the first line has 5 syllables, the second has 7, and the last has 5.

When writing haiku, it is considered traditional to include a kigo, or "season word," to place the poem in a seasonal context and connect it to the temporal, cyclical aspect of nature; however, a kigo is not absolutely required.

One of the hallmarks of haiku is its sense of immediacy: haiku is all about the present moment, and the essence of that moment, whether ordinary or extraordinary.

One of the greatest female Japanese haiku poets was Chiyo-ni, who lived from 1703 to 1775. The daughter of a picture framer, she became the disciple of the famous poet Basho when she was 12. By 17 her poetry was well known throughout Japan. Her most famous poem is "Morning Glory."

A morning glory.
Twined round the bucket:
I will ask my neighbor for water.

Explorers

ALEXANDRA DAVID-NÉEL

Alexandra David-Néel, born Louise Eugénie Alexandrine Marie David (1868–1969), was the first European woman to travel to the forbidden city of Lhasa, Tibet, in 1924, when it was still closed to foreigners. She was a French explorer, spiritualist, Buddhist, and writer, penning over thirty books on Eastern religion, philosophy, and the experiences she had on her travels. By the time she was eighteen, she had already made solo trips to England, Spain, and Switzerland, and when she was twenty-two, she went to India, returning to France only when she

Alexandra David-Néel

ran out of money. She married railroad engineer Philippe Néel in 1904, and in 1911 she returned to India to study Buddhism at the royal monastery of Sikkim, where she met the Crown Prince Sidkeon Tulku. In 1912 she met the thirteenth Dalai Lama twice and was able to ask him questions about Buddhism. She deepened her study of spirituality when she spent two years living in a cave in Sikkim, near the Tibetan border. It was there that she met the young Sikkimese monk Aphur Yongden, who became her lifelong traveling companion, and whom she would later adopt. The two trespassed into Tibetan territory in 1916, meeting the Panchen Lama, but were evicted by British authorities. They left for Japan, traveled through China, and in 1924 arrived in Lhasa, Tibet, disguised as pilgrims. They lived there for two months. In 1928, Alexandra separated from her husband and settled in Digne, France, where she spent the next ten years writing books about her adventures. She reconciled with her husband and traveled again with her adopted son in 1937, at age sixty-nine, going through the Soviet Union to China, India, and eventually Tachienlu, where she continued her study of Tibetan literature. It was an arduous journey that took nearly ten years to complete. She returned to Digne in 1946 to settle the estate of her husband, who had died in 1941, and again wrote books and gave lectures about what she had seen. Her last camping trip, at an Alpine lake in early winter, 2,240 meters above sea level, was at age eighty-two. She lived to be 100, dying just eighteen days before her 101st birthday.

FREYA STARK

Dame Freya Madeleine Stark (1893-1993) was a British travel writer, explorer, and cartographer. She was one of the first Western women to travel the Arabian deserts, and was fluent in Arabic and several other languages. She traveled to Turkey, the Middle East, Greece, and Italy, but her passion was the Middle East. When she was

Freya Stark

thirty-five, she explored the forbidden territory of the Syrian Druze, traveling through "The Valley of the Assassins" before being thrown into a military prison. In the 1930s, she went to the outback of southern Arabia, where few Westerners had explored, and discovered the hidden routes of the ancient incense trade. During World War II, she joined the Ministry of Information and helped create propaganda to encourage Arabic support of the Allies. Even in her sixties, she continued her travels, retracing Alexander the Great's journeys into Asia and writing three more books based on those trips. By the time of her death, at age 100, she had written two dozen books on her adventures.

FLORENCE BAKER

Lady Florence Baker (1841-1916), was born Barbara Maria Szász. She was orphaned at seven, and at age seventeen she was due to be sold at an Ottoman slave market in Hungary when a thirty-eight-year-old English widower, Sam Baker, paid for her and rescued her from her captors. She was renamed Florence, and years later she became Samuel Baker's wife. They were a perfect match: Sam was an established explorer,

Florence Baker

and Florence a natural-born adventurer, and so the two of them traveled to Africa, searching for the source of the Nile and shooting big game. They managed to reach the secondary source of the Nile, which they called Lake Albert in honor of Queen Victoria's recently deceased husband, and then in 1865 they made the journey to Britain, where they married (and where she met her stepchildren, Sam's children by his first wife) and where Sam received a knighthood. They returned to Africa in 1870 to report on the slave trade along the Nile. Later they journeyed to India and Japan before returning to Britain. Florence outlived Sam by twenty-three years and was cared for in her old age by her stepchildren.

A TIMELINE OF WOMEN EXPLORERS

1704   Sarah Kemble Knight journeys on horseback, solo, from Boston to New York.

1876   Maria Spelternia is the first woman to cross Niagara Falls on a high wire.

1895   Annie Smith Peck becomes the first woman to climb the Matterhorn.

1901   Annie Taylor is the first person to go over Niagara Falls in a barrel.

1926   Gertrude Ederle is the first woman to swim the English Channel.

1947   Barbara Washburn becomes the first woman to climb Mt. McKinley.

1975   Junko Tabei of Japan is the first woman to climb Mt. Everest.

1976   Krystyna Choynowski-Liskiewicz of Poland is the first woman to sail around the world solo.

1979   Sylvia Earle is the first person in the world to dive to a depth of 1,250 feet.

1983   Sally Ride becomes the first American woman in space.

1984   Cosmonaut Svetlana Savitskaya becomes the first woman to walk in space.

1985   Tania Aebi, at nineteen, becomes the youngest person ever to sail alone around the world.

1985   Libby Riddles is the first woman to win the Iditarod Dog-Sled Race in Alaska.

1986   American Ann Bancroft becomes the first woman in the world to ski to the North Pole.

2001   Ann Bancroft and Norwegian Liv Arnesen are the first women to cross Antarctica on skis.

2005 Ellen MacArthur breaks the world's record for sailing solo around the world.

2007 Eighteen-year-old Samantha Larson becomes the youngest American to climb Mt. Everest and also the youngest person to climb the Seven Summits. (She and her father, Dr. David Larson, are the first father-daughter team to complete the Seven Summits.)

All About Zero

Zero is a mysterious number. It is nothing, absence, emptiness. But it is also something: a placeholder, a marker, a separator. Zero has the distinction of being both a thing and an idea, a quality and a quantity. Here are some amazing facts about zero.

WORDS FOR ZERO AROUND THE WORLD

In French, it is *zéro*. In Italian, the word zero began as *zefiro,* which resembles the Latin and Greek words *zephyrus* and *zephyrum,* all meaning "west wind." In Arabic, zero is *sifr,* which evolved from the words *cifra,* and *safira* ("it was empty"); our word *cipher* is a descendant of these terms as well. In German, zero is *null.* And in Sanskrit zero is *śūnya* ("void" or "empty"). English has many words for zero: aught, blank, cipher, dud, dummy, goose egg, nada, nadir, naught, nil, nix, nothing, null, void, and zilch, to name a few.

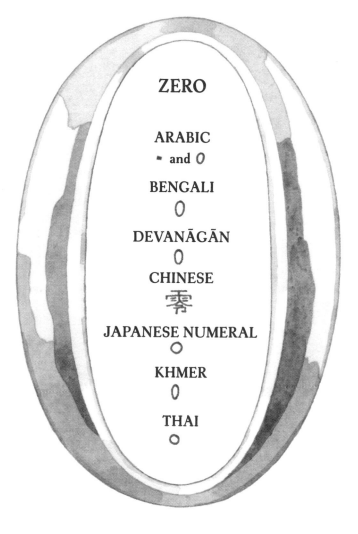

ZERO

ARABIC
٠ and 0

BENGALI
0

DEVANĀGĀN
0

CHINESE
零

JAPANESE NUMERAL
0

KHMER
0

THAI
0

ZERO IN HISTORY

○ The ancient Chinese, Egyptians, and Greeks did not have a symbol for zero.

○ No one knows who invented zero, but some of the earliest examples of zero being used as a placeholder (distinguishing, say, 29 from 209) were found in Babylonian cuneiform tablets dating from around 300 or 400 BC.

○ Interestingly, however, the Babylonians had used a mathematical system without zero for over a thousand years before they hit upon the idea of zero.

○ The idea of zero as a number (rather than just a placeholder) was developed in India around the fifth century.

○ The Italian mathematician Leonardo Fibonnaci, who grew up in North Africa and studied Arabic and Hindu mathematics, introduced the concept of zero (which he called *zephyrum*) to Europe in the 12th century. (For more on Fibonnaci, see page 176.)

FASCINATING FACTS

- On a roulette wheel, which features numbers 1 through 36 in alternating red and black, the number zero is green. (American roulette wheels even have a second green spot—marked double-zero, 00.)

- In tennis, a score of zero is called "love"—from the French *l'oeuf,* or egg, because of the way zero resembles an egg-shape. In other sports, too, you may have noticed announcers referring to a score of zero as "a big goose egg."

- A tarot card deck has 22 "trump" cards decorated with illustrations of people and symbolic scenes. Card number zero is "The Fool." The Fool is usually depicted as a ragged but happy vagabond with tattered clothes and a stick on his back carrying all his worldly possessions. And rather than being "foolish" in the way we think of the world, he is meant to symbolize child-like wonder and curiosity, and the endless possibility of experience.

○ On telephones, the zero comes after the number 9 instead of before the number 1. When it is pressed by itself, and not within a sequence of other numbers, it summons the operator. (Long ago, that was an actual person operating the connections between telephone lines; nowadays pressing zero will route you to a computerized menu of options for helping you make your call.)

○ Anton Bruckner and Alfred Schnittke are the only composers of classical music to write a symphony titled Symphony No. 0. Bruckner also wrote a symphony called Symphony No. 00.

ZERO, THE SPOOKY COINCIDENCE, AND TECUMSEH'S CURSE

Tecumseh (whose name means "he who walks across the sky") was a Shawnee leader who rallied Native American tribes to defend their land in the early 1800s. During the Battle of Tippecanoe in 1811, he was killed by troops commanded by military leader William Henry Harrison.

Harrison went on to become the ninth president of the United States—but he died of pneumonia only thirty-one days into his term. It is the briefest term in history, and he was the first president to die while in office.

A legend has grown up around this series of events, called "the zero factor," or "Tecumseh's Curse." The story has it that Tecumseh's brother placed a curse on Harrison, and in fact on every president elected in a year ending in the number zero: They would all be doomed to die in office.

If we go along with the premise that a curse was indeed made, it seems to have had a remarkably long run in terms of accuracy. Harrison was elected in 1840 and died after just 31 days. Presidents Lincoln (1860), Garfield (1880), and McKinley (elected to a second term in 1900) were all assassinated. Harding (1920) died of a stroke. Roosevelt (elected to a third term in 1940) died of a cerebral hemorrhage. Kennedy (1960) was assassinated.

But Ronald Reagan, who was elected in 1980, survived an assassination attempt, and George W. Bush, who was first elected in 2000, has escaped the curse unscathed. But we will have to wait until the elections of 2020 to see if the curse has finally been lifted.

Negotiate a Salary
FOR DOG-WALKING, ERRAND-RUNNING, BABYSITTING—OR ANYTHING!

Let us never negotiate out of fear, but let us never fear to negotiate.
—John F. Kennedy, Inaugural Address, 1961.

The word "negotiate" comes from the Latin word *negotiari,* meaning "to trade." When you negotiate something, you are essentially asking for someone to trade you something, and making a case for why that would be a good idea. There are several steps to a successful negotiation: preparation, presentation, contemplation, and sealing the deal.

PREPARATION
Define your goals. Do you want a higher salary? Do you want more hours? Do you want to be paid extra for overtime? Narrowing down what it is you want will help you approach the task of asking for it.

Do your research. Find out what the going rate is in your neighborhood for the work you do—how much do your friends get paid for the same work? Does the amount they get depend on the level of responsibility they have? Once you know the answers to these questions, you'll know the facts about what other people are paid, and you'll be better prepared to ask for what you want.

PRESENTATION

Plan what you're going to say and how you're going to say it.

Begin with lower-priority requests, if possible, and work your way up to the big ones. (When you get to the big request, you can trade off some of the lower-priority requests if necessary.)

Accentuate the positive. This is not the time for modesty—emphasize your accomplishments and abilities and point out why it is you deserve what you are asking for. Smile, be confident, and be friendly.

CONTEMPLATION

Listen. Sometimes the most important part of a conversation is the part when you're not talking. When it's time for the other person to respond, listen carefully to what he or she has to say.

Think. You may be presented with a counteroffer—an offer made in response to your offer. You don't have to respond to a counteroffer right away. You can take your time and think about it, even if that means not giving your answer for a few days.

SEALING THE DEAL

Sign on the dotted line. Once both parties have reached an agreement, it's a good idea to put that final offer in writing, and have both of you sign the document. This will prevent any future misunderstandings or miscommunications about what was actually agreed upon during your negotiation. Still, sometimes a good old-fashioned handshake will do.

COMMON MISTAKES

Not preparing. Make sure you have done your research and know what you are talking about. If you're not sure, postpone the negotiation until you've had time to get ready.

Trying to win at all costs. Arguing or using intimidating behavior is going to hinder rather than help the negotia-

TIPS

Even though it might make you nervous to ask for something, whether it's a higher salary or more responsibility, it's important to try to maintain an open and confident attitude. You want to make the person you're negotiating with want to say yes to you—and it's very hard to say no to a smiling, friendly person. Some people call this technique to "disarm with charm." But whether or not you're good at being "charming," try to smile, look people directly in the eye, and concentrate on not speaking too fast. Remember, this is just a conversation! You have those all the time. (Also, the people you're negotiating with may expect you to be nervous or insecure about the negotiation process—so acting comfortable and confident may catch them off guard and make them even more likely to say yes to your request.)

tion process. Remember, the central process of negotiation is discussion with others to reach an agreement or compromise. It's a dialogue, not a monologue.

Talking too much. Listen carefully to what the other person has to say, and when it's your turn to speak, be direct and to the point.

Trying to be someone you're not. The key in negotiation is to be comfortable. If you are trying to act "tough" because you think it will make the discussion go your way, you may be sadly disappointed. Being the most confident version of yourself is better than trying to be the kind of person you think you should be in order to win.

Abigail Adams' Letters with John Adams

Letter writing, real letter writing, is a storied part of American life. Friends and spouses built relationships, and political thinkers changed the world, by expressing their thoughts and sending them through the mail.

The correspondence between Abigail Adams and John Adams during the American Revolution tops the list of our country's famous letter writing, both for the couple's modern relationship and the important political events they discussed. The relationship was modern because John so valued the opinions of Abigail, who was well educated and believed learned women had much to contribute to society. The events they discussed were so important because they shaped the birth of our nation, and John would later become the second President of the United States.

Abigail Adams, born Abigail Smith, came of age as a member of the wealthy Smiths of Massachusetts Bay Colony, related to the Quincys on her mother's side. Many generations of men in her family had studied at Harvard, but, as the college didn't accept girls, Abigail's mother and grandmother tutored her at home in math, literature, and writing.

John Adams was the son of a shoemaker from Braintree, Massachusetts, and his mother helped run their family's farm. He earned a law degree from Harvard. They met because Abigail's sister Mary courted and then married John's close friend Richard Cranch. Several years later, in 1764, John and Abigail married; Abigail was a few days shy of twenty, and John, several years older, had just turned twenty-nine.

John's passion for reading, like Abigail's, drew them together, and they formed an extraordinary bond. They pored over important books of the time, by such authors as Adam Smith, Mary Wollstonecraft, and Jean-Jacques Rousseau, discussing them at length and, at least on John's part, making voluminous comments in the margins. As John grew more involved in public life, the couple developed relationships with important thinkers, including Abigail's famous friendship with Mercy Otis Warren, who lived in nearby Plymouth and documented the American Revolution.

Between the years 1774 and 1783, John spent long stretches away from Abigail. He worked with the Continental Congress in Philadelphia to draft the Declaration of Independence. He went to France to join Benjamin Franklin in crafting the Treaty of Paris, which ended the War for Independence (also known as the American Revolution). Abigail stayed in Massachusetts to tend their four children and their home.

During this period, Franklin was the Postmaster General, multiplying post offices and introducing the stagecoach as a means of delivering mail reliably between the emerging States. John and Abigail made good use of this new postal system. We know of 284 letters between them from this time, thanks to their grandson, Charles Francis Adams, who kept and edited the letters, releasing them for the nation's centennial in 1876. Throughout their lives, they wrote more than 1,100 letters to each other.

John to Abigail, Philadelphia, 29 March 1776

I give you joy of Boston and Charlestown, once more the Habitations of Americans. Am waiting with great Impatience for Letters from you, which I know will contain many Particulars. We are taking Precautions to defend every Place that is in [Danger]—The Carolinas, Virginia, N. York, Canada. I can think of nothing but fortifying Boston Harbour.

Abigail to John, Braintree, 31 March 1776

I long to hear that you have declared an independency— and, by the way in the new Code of Laws which I suppose it will be necessary for you to make I desire you would Remember the Ladies, and be more generous and favourable to them than your ancestors. Do not put such unlimited power in the hands of the Husbands . . . That your Sex are Naturally Tyrannical is a Truth so thoroughly established as to admit of no dispute, but such of you as wish to be happy willingly give up the harsh title of Master for the more tender and endearing one of Friend.

John to Abigail, Philadelphia, 3 July 1776

Your Favour of June 17 dated at Plymouth, was handed me, by yesterday's Post. I was much pleased to find that you had taken a journey to Plymouth, to see your Friends in the long Absence of one whom you may wish to see. The Excursion will be an Amusement, and will serve your Health. How happy would it have made me to have taken this journey with you?

Yesterday the greatest Question was decided, which ever was debated in America, and a greater perhaps, never was or will be decided among Men. A Resolution was passed without one dissenting Colony "that these united Colonies, are, and of right ought to be free and independent States, and as such, they have, and of Right ought to have full Power to make War, conclude Peace, establish Commerce, and to do all the other Acts and Things, which other States may rightfully do." You will see in a few days a Declaration setting forth the Causes, which have impell'd Us to this mighty Revolution, and the Reasons which will justify it, in the Sight of God and Man. A Plan of Confederation will be taken up in a few days.

Abigail to John, Boston, Sunday, 14 July 1776

By yesterday's post I received two Letters dated 3 and 4 of July and tho your Letters never fail to give me pleasure, be the subject what it will, yet it was greatly heightened by the prospect of the future happiness and glory of our Country; nor am I a little Gratified when I reflect that a person so nearly connected with me has had the Honour of being a principal actor, in laying a foundation for its future Greatness. May the foundation of our new constitution, be justice, Truth and Righteousness. Like the wise Mans house may it be founded upon those Rocks and then neither storms or tempests will overthrow it. . . . all our Friends desire to be rememberd to you and foremost in that Number stands your Portia.*

* The wife of the Roman Republican Senator, Brutus. Abigail often signed her letters with that name.

Tide Charts

Every beach on the planet has a unique cycle of tides, and thus its own tide chart. Look for one in the local newspaper, or at a nearby marina or surf shop.

Tide charts help you pick the best times to go fishing, crabbing, or surfing. When you are boating, it helps to know what the water is doing, as paddling a canoe into a creek when the tide is trending low is a great deal harder than, say, swooping in with the rush of a coming high tide.

Tide charts come in different forms. Once you know the basics of high and low tide, water height, and moon phases, you'll be able to read any tide chart.

The tide chart in this illustration predicts nine days of tides. This is a high tide chart because it's primarily for fishing. When you fish, you wake up in the morning and before even opening your eyes you wonder, "When's high tide?" High tide is when the fish are out and moving, whether on the incoming flood tide or the outgoing ebb tide. At least that's what you hope. A small-print note at the bottom of this chart mentions that low tide comes about six hours later.

LIFE GUARD ON DUTY

Striped bass are running today!

Day	A.M.	P.M.
Mon.	4:25	5:02
Tues. ∫	5:19	5:51
Wed.	6:17	6:43
Thur.	7:17	7:36
Fri	8:15	8:28
Sat	9:08	9:20
Sun	9:59	10:11

Low tide: add 6 hours

∫ first quarter moon

✦ full moon

✦ new moon   ▣ ¾ moon

Notice several things. First, high tide comes 50-60 minutes later each day. The tidal day is slightly longer than our regular 24-hour day, at 24 hours and 50 minutes. (Why? Because our regular days rely on the earth rotating around the sun, and tidal days rely on the moon rotating around the earth, which takes 50 minutes longer.)

Second, the tide chart lists the phases of the moon. During the first few days the moon will wax to a first-quarter crescent. The moon will be full six or seven days later and with any luck it will be a bulgingly orange late-summer moon, rising low and pumpkin-like in the sky.

Tide charts show the moon phases because tides are caused by the pull of the moon's gravity—and the sun's gravity—on earth's water. It's an awe-inspiring concept that the moon's pull—even at 239,000 miles away—is so strong that it can control our ocean waters. Next time you are at the seashore, with the waves lapping at your feet, you can observe the power of the moon.

More practically, tide charts list moon phases because it matters when you go fishing. High tides are higher during the new moon and the full moon. These are called spring tides. People who fish don't much like spring tides—the water level is higher, and silt and sand from the bottom churn up and make the water murky. The result: Fish can't see the bait on your line, and that's no good if you're trying to catch them. Some people will plan their fishing trips way in advance using the moon phases of tide charts, knowing to avoid the few days around new and full moon.

The opposite of high water spring tides are neap tides. They happen during the first and third quarters, when the moon waxes and wanes. There's less water at high tide, and slightly less current.

There are two more moon trivia words you'll want to know: a crescent moon is anything less than half, and any phase slightly-more-than-half to just-under-whole is a gibbous moon.

CRABBING: A CAPE COD TIDE CHART

Date	Day	Time	Height	Time	Height	Time	Height	Time	Height
7/10/07	Mon	5:18 AM	0.0 L	11:10 AM	2.1 H	5:09 PM	0.4 L	11:24 PM	3.1 H

This chart shows low tide, which makes it helpful for crabbing and beachcombing. The initial *Time* column lists the first tide after midnight, no matter whether it's low or high. Set your alarm clock, because that first tide comes in at 5:18 in the morning. The next column, *Height,* tells that the height of the water is 0.0, or average water level, and that the tide is L, or low. If you're not an early riser, look for the second low tide of the day. Reading from left to right, you'll see a high tide at 11:10 A.M., and then another low tide at 5:09 P.M. That's the one you want.

At 4:00, then, head for the beach. The hours just before and after low tide are especially good for beachcombing and crabbing. Low tide is also a good time to see birds along the shore. They'll be there picking at small animals and crabs that were left on the beach after the water receded.

SURFING: A COSTA RICAN TIDE CHART

Date	Day	Time	Height	Time	Height	Time	Height	Time	Height
7/10/07	Mon	5:18 AM	0.0 L	11:10 AM	2.1 H	5:09 PM	0.4 L	11:24 PM	3.1 H

This chart from Nosara, on the Pacific coast of Costa Rica shows the tides in 24-hour time, which is used throughout the world, especially in non-English-speaking nations. (In the United States, 24-hour time is called

Military Time, since that's where it's most often used.)

Hours 13–24 are equivalent to 1 P.M.–12 A.M. on the 12-hour clock, so to convert, just subtract 12. Thus high tide at 16:13 is 4:13 P.M., and low tide at 22:21 is 10:21 P.M.

Globe-trotting surfers, even American ones, must get used to 24-hour time so they can easily read the tide charts as they travel across continents, surfboard under arm, seeking the perfect wave. This chart does a great job of showing how high the waves will swell. For surfing, the combination of tide, wind, and swell determine whether any given surf spot, or break, will have rideable waves at any given hour.

For example, a reef break means the waves are created (or break) when incoming water hits a reef that comes up from the ocean floor. At low tide, a reef break may give an excellent ride, on fast, steep waves. At high tide, however, the water may be so deep that it does not make strong impact with the reef, and this results in barely any wave to ride at all.

On the other hand, a beach break means waves form off large sandbars underwater. Often a higher tide is best for these surf spots, because they need the force of a lot of water rushing over the sandbars to make long, rounded waves.

BOATING: A CALIFORNIA TIDE CHART

By now you're an old hand at reading charts. The last chart comes from Half Moon Bay, California. It includes longitude (37.5017° N) and latitude (122.4866° W), which you'll want to know if you're taking a boat out on the Pacific Ocean and using your navigation equipment to find your way back to shore.

The chart also gives times for sunrise and sunset, so you can get out on the water early and you'll know when you'd best return to the marina before nightfall. Notice, too, how the date is notated, as year-month-day; that's standard tide-chart notation.

Tuesday 2007-07-03			
Sunrise	5:53 AM	Sunset	8:34 PM
Moonrise	11:04 PM	Moonset	9:00 AM
High Tide		12:13 AM	5.76 feet
Low Tide		7:22 AM	-1.00 feet
High Tide		2:29 PM	4.59 feet
Low Tide		7:23 PM	2.93 feet

Emily Dickinson

Emily Dickinson lived from 1830 to 1886 in Amherst, Massachusetts. She was a private person (her reclusive nature was the focus of the Tony Award-winning play about her, "The Belle of Amherst"), but she left the world an incredible legacy of poetry exploring life, love, philosophy, nature, and the human spirit. Her poetry was sharply dissimilar to the poetry written around that time, with her creative use of punctuation and the way her work veered between poetry and prose. She wrote to express herself and to make sense of the world around her—one particularly intense year saw her writing 300 poems!—and was  encouraged in her literary efforts by a mentor at the *Atlantic Monthly* who pronounced her a "wholly new and poetic genius." Still, only seven of her poems were published during her lifetime, and anonymously at that, so she never lived to see the critical response her poetry generated. Now she is held alongside Walt Whitman as one of the two great founders of the American poetic tradition. Here are seven of her most famous poems.

Hope is the thing with feathers—
That perches in the soul—
And sings the tune without the words—
And never stops—at all—

And sweetest—in the gale—is heard; —
And sore must be the storm—
That could abash the little bird
That kept so many warm—

I've heard it in the chillest land—
And on the strangest sea—
Yet, never, in extremity,
It asked a crumb—of me.

I'm nobody! Who are you?
Are you—nobody—too?
Then there's a pair of us—don't tell!
They'd banish us—you know.
How dreary—to be—somebody!
How public—like a frog—
To tell your name—the livelong day—
To an admiring bog!

My life closed twice before its close—
It yet remains to see
If Immortality unveil
A third event to me.

So huge, so hopeless to conceive,
As these that twice befell.
Parting is all we know of heaven,
And all we need of hell.

EMILY DICKINSON

This is my letter to the World
That never wrote to Me—
The simple News that Nature told—
With tender Majesty
Her Message is committed
To Hands I cannot see—
For love of Her—Sweet countrymen—
Judge tenderly—of Me.

There is no frigate like a book
To take us lands away,
Nor any coursers like a page
Of prancing poetry—

This traverse may the poorest take
Without oppress of toll—
How frugal is the chariot
That bears a human soul!

EMILY DICKINSON

I dwell in Possibility—
A fairer House than Prose—
More numerous of Windows—
Superior—for Doors—
Of Chambers as the Cedars—
Impregnable of Eye—
And for an Everlasting Roof
The Gambrels of the Sky—

Of Visitors—the fairest—
For Occupation—This—
The spreading wide my narrow Hands
To gather Paradise—

Because I could not stop for Death—
He kindly stopped for me—
The Carriage held but just Ourselves—
And Immortality.

We slowly drove—He knew no haste
And I had put away

My labour and my leisure too,
For His Civility—
We passed the School, where Children strove
At Recess—in the Ring—
We passed the Fields of Gazing Grain—
We passed the Setting Sun—

Or rather—He passed Us—
The Dews drew quivering and chill—
For only Gossamer, my Gown—
My Tippet—only Tulle—

We paused before a House that seemed
A Swelling of the Ground—
The Roof was scarcely visible—
The Cornice—in the Ground—

Since then—'tis Centuries—and yet
Feels shorter than the Day
I first surmised the Horses Heads
Were toward Eternity—

EMILY DICKINSON

Queens of the Ancient World: Salome Alexandra of Judea

S alome's story is a tale of diplomacy, of managing the constant challenges of royal leadership, and of resisting attacks from outside armies as well as from members of her own family. She is remembered as the last independent ruler of her country, Judea, during the period just before the countries of the Mediterranean were conquered by Rome.

Salome Alexandra was born in 140 BC. Not much is known of her girlhood. Her Judean name was Shelamzion, which is translated as Salome. Her Greek name was Alexandra, after Alexander the Great, who brought his Greek armies to the region nearly 200 years earlier. Like many people of her time, Salome lived amid her family and clan and spoke their language, Aramaic. She was also versed in the Hellenistic culture and Greek language that united the many lands around the Mediterranean Sea, including the nearby empires of Egypt and Syria.

From what historians can piece together, it seems Salome Alexandra first married in her late twenties. Her choice of husband—Aristobulus, the eldest son of the native ruler of Judea—led her both to royal life and to the beginning of her family problems. Aristobulus was intensely ambitious. When his father the king died in 104 BC, he willed the country to Aristobulus' mother. But his eldest son would have none of it. He imprisoned his mother, starved her to death, and jailed three of his brothers.

In this brutal way, Judea became his, and Salome became the reigning queen. Just a year later, though, Aristobulus died of a mysterious disease. As Salome performed the proper funeral rites over him, she learned that he had bequeathed the kingdom to her.

Salome was faced with another complicated decision: should she rule by herself or share the throne? She released the three royal brothers from jail and chose the eldest of them to be king and high priest. His name was Alexander Janneus. She married him and continued her life as queen.

Her second husband, Alexander, was a tough man to live with. He was mean-tempered and he drank too much. He was fond of raiding and pillaging nearby cities, and he was cruel to his own people. He reigned for twenty-seven years. The historian Josephus tells us that as much as the people hated Alexander, they adored Salome, and considered her wise, kind, strong and reliable, decent, fair, and a person of good judgment. It's possible that during Alexander's long rule, the people didn't rise to overthrow him because they loved Salome so much.

In 76 BC, Alexander was on his deathbed. He called Salome close and bequeathed the kingdom to her, returning the favor she had granted him twenty-seven years before.

Alexander presented Salome with a plan: "Conceal my death until, under your command, the soldiers will have won this battle we are now fighting. March back to the capital Jerusalem and hold a Victory. I have oppressed many people, and they now hate me. Make peace with them. Tell them you will include their leaders as advisors in your government. Finally, when you return to Jerusalem, send for the leading men. Show them my dead body and give it over to them. Let them defile it, if they wish, or honor me with a proper burial. The choice will be theirs. And then, they will support you." Quite a beginning for the new reigning queen.

As queen, ruling from her palace in Jerusalem, Salome faced immediate challenges from her family once more, this time from her two grown sons. Salome anointed her oldest son, Hyrcanus, a quieter and more private sort of man, to be high priest. Hebrew religious law forbade women from overseeing the Temple and performing the animal sacrifices, so although she was queen, she couldn't be high priest, as her husband had been. Her younger son, named Aristobulus after Salome's first ruthless husband, was a much bigger problem. Like his father, he was very ambitious. He wanted Salome's throne from the start. Soon he would rise against her.

True to her promises and King Alexander's plan, Salome delegated the domestic affairs and a good deal of the power over the nation's religious life to the elders of Judea. This helped to end the civil war that had simmered under her husband's rule, during which he had killed a great many of the elders' group. Still, the remaining elders wanted revenge. Before Salome could stop them, they slit the throat of one of Alexander's ringleaders, Diogenes, and set out to find more.

The ambitious son Aristobulus used the growing violence to threaten his mother's reign. After the revenge killings, Aristobulus led a delegation of men to Salome's throne. They demanded she put a stop to the killings. If she could do so, they promised they would not avenge the recent murders. They would keep the country from descending into a spiral of violence. In return for keeping the peace, Aristobulus demanded his mother give him several of the family fortresses strung throughout the desert from Jerusalem to the Jordan River.

Salome negotiated a deal. She kept the majority of the fortresses for herself, including those that housed her royal treasure, but she gave a few to Aristobulus. Seeking to push him far from her capital, she dispatched him on a small military mission to Damascus.

As Salome dealt with the situation at home, another problem was brewing outside of Judea. The country's northern neighbor, Syria, was very weak. The Seleucid dynasty that had once controlled the entire region was in its last days. Taking advantage of this weakness, King Tigranes of

Armenia descended on Syria with a massive army of a half million soldiers, quickly taking over Syria's cities. Tigranes trapped the Syrian queen, Cleopatra Selene, in the city of Ptolemais, on the Mediterranean coast.

Ptolemais was not far from Salome's city of Jerusalem. Terrible news of the siege reached Salome quickly, as did the rumor that Tigranes planned to march on Judea next. Salome knew that despite her large army of mercenaries and native soldiers, she could not beat Tigranes.

Rather than ready her troops for war, Queen Salome took a different stance. She sent her ambassadors to meet with King Tigranes, and sent along with them many camels loaded with extraordinary treasure. Tigranes agreed not to attack. Luck was on Salome's side, because another army had begun to attack Armenia. Instead of marching south toward Jerusalem, Tigranes had to turn north to defend his own people back home.

That episode, and the years of strife leading up to it, wore Salome down. She was over seventy, and her health was beginning to fail. She had outlived two husbands, she faced attacks from outsiders, and her youngest son continued to undermine her authority from within.

Sensing her final frailty, Aristobulus planned a coup. He had been angry that Salome negotiated a peace with King Tigranes. Had it been up to him, he would have led their soldiers to battle. He knew she was near death, and he suspected that she would bequeath the throne to his older brother, who was already the high priest.

Secretly, Aristobulus left the family palace in Jerusalem. He rode his horse through the countryside, and at each city and village he asked the people to foreswear their allegiance to Queen Salome and pledge their loyalty to him.

Salome gathered her last ounce of strength and decided to take harsh action against her son. She imprisoned his wife and children—much as her first husband had done to his relatives. She stashed them in a fortress next to the Temple where Hyrcanus was high priest, but she knew her time was running out. She gave Hyrcanus the keys to the treasury and directed him to take command of her army.

Salome Alexandra died soon thereafter, in 67 BC, before Aristobulus could strike against her. She was seventy-three, had reigned for nine years as her people's only independent queen, and she died a natural death. Salome took part in no great battles. She commanded no stunning ships on the sea. She merely did her best to keep the peace at home and to keep stronger armies at bay.

Queen Salome was so admired that for many generations, hers was one of the two most popular names that Judean people would give to their baby daughters (including one infamous Salome who appears in the New Testament). She couldn't have known that she would be the only Judean queen, and that this era of independent states was about to end.

In the year Salome died, across the sea in Italy an empire was growing. The Roman general Pompey was fighting the pirates who controlled the Mediterranean. He cleared them out and made it safe once again to cross the vast waters by boat. By 64 BC, Pompey forged his soldiers into battalions and started his eastward trek. He took control of Syria later that year, and of Judea the year after. Soon, all of western Asia was under Rome's hand, and the era of Queen Salome the diplomat was a distant memory.

Clouds

The terms for categorizing clouds were developed by Luke Howard, a London pharmacist and amateur meteorologist, in the early 1800s. Before this, clouds were merely described by how they appeared to the viewer: gray, puffy, fleece, towers and castles, white, dark. Shortly before Howard came up with his cloud names, a few other weather scientists started devising cloud terminology of their own. But it was ultimately Howard's names, based on Latin descriptive terms, that stuck.

Howard named three main types of clouds: cumulus, stratus, and cirrus. Clouds that carried precipitation he called "nimbus," the Latin word for rain.

Cumulus is Latin for "heap" or "pile," so it makes sense that cumulus clouds are recognizable by their puffy cotton-ball-like appearance. These types of clouds are formed when warm and

moist air is pushed upward, and their size depends on the force of that upward movement and the amount of water in the air. Cumulus clouds that are full of rain are called cumulonimbus.

Stratus clouds are named for their layered, flat, stretched-out appearance, as "stratus" is the Latin word for layer. These clouds can look like a huge blanket across the sky.

Cirrus clouds are named for their wispy, feathery look. "Cirrus" means "curl of hair," and looking at cirrus clouds you can see why Luke Howard thought to describe them that way. These clouds form only at high altitudes and are so thin that sunlight can pass all the way through them.

Nimbus clouds, the rain clouds, can have any structure, or none at all. If you've seen the sky on a rainy day and it looks like one big giant grey cloud, you'll know what we mean.

Spies

UNLIKELY SPIES

Julia Child

Before she became a famous chef, Julia Child was a spy. She worked for the Office of Strategic Services, a precursor of the CIA, and went undercover to Sri Lanka (called Ceylon at the time) with top security clearance. In World War II, she helped the U.S. Navy solve their problem with sharks—who had a habit of setting off underwater explosive devices, foiling U.S. plans to blow up German U-boats—by developing shark repellent. She met diplomat Paul Child when she was working for the OSS, and they married. When Paul was posted to Paris, Julia trained at the famous Cordon Bleu cooking school and began her second life as a chef.

Hedy Lamarr

Hedwig Eva Maria Kiesler is best known as Hedy Lamarr, movie star of the 1930s and '40s. But she was also an inventor who patented an idea that was to become the key to modern wireless communication. During World War II, Hedy, along with George Antheil, invented a way to make military communications secure through frequency-hopping, an early form of a technology called spread spectrum. Hedy's status as a beautiful and successful actress provided her with the perfect cover: she was able to visit a variety of venues on tour

Hedy Lamarr

and interact with many people, none of whom suspected that the stunning starlet might be listening closely and thinking of ways to help the U.S. cause.

Josephine Baker

Josephine Baker was another World War II-era entertainer whose celebrity status helped distract from her mission as a spy. Josephine was an African American dancer and singer from St. Louis, Missouri. She found some success in the United States, but was hindered by racial prejudice. She moved to Paris when she was nineteen and became an international star. When World

Josephine Baker

War II began, she started working as an undercover operative for the French Resistance, transporting orders and maps from the Resistance into countries occupied by Germany. Her fame and renown made it easy for her to pass unsuspected, as foreign officials were thrilled to meet such a famous performer, but she wrote the secret information in disappearing ink on her sheet music just in case.

The Girl Guides

During the First World War, the Girl Guides—the British version of Girl Scouts—were used as couriers for secret messages by MI-5, Britain's counter-intelligence agency. Messengers were needed to work in the War Office at the time, and at first Boy Scouts were used. But they proved to be difficult to manage, so Girl Guides were asked to serve instead. The girls, most of whom were between fourteen and eighteen years old, ran messages and patrolled on the roof; for their efforts they were paid ten shillings a week, plus food. Like all employees of MI-5, they took a pledge of secrecy. But unlike many employees of MI-5, they were among the least likely spies to arouse suspicion.

REVOLUTIONARY WAR SPIES

During the Revolutionary War, many women up and down the East Coast passed important information along to General Washington at Valley Forge. Philadelphian Lydia Barrington Darragh spied on the British for American officers. Two Loyalists (citizens loyal to Britain), "Miss Jenny" and Ann Bates, spied on the Americans for the British. Ann Trotter Bailey carried messages across enemy territory in 1774, as did Sarah Bradlee Fulton, nicknamed the "mother of the Boston Tea Party"; Emily Geiger rode fifty miles through enemy territory to deliver information to General Sumter. The anonymous spy "355"—a numerical code that meant "lady" or "woman"—was a member of the Culper Ring, a New York–based secret spy organization. She was seized by the British in 1780 and died on a prison ship—but not before she named Benedict Arnold as a potential traitor.

CIVIL WAR SPIES

Pauline Cushman was an actress who worked as a Union spy. She was captured with incriminating papers and sentenced to be executed, but was rescued just three days prior to her hanging. President Abraham Lincoln gave her the honorary commission of Major, and she toured the country for years, telling of her exploits spying for the Union.

Mary Elizabeth Bowser was a freed slave who served as a maid in the Confederate White House. Her servile status—and the mistaken assumption that she could neither read nor write—allowed her to be present for key conversations but largely ignored. She smuggled important information and papers to the Union Army.

Sarah Emma Edmonds disguised herself as a man so that she could serve in the Union Army, where she became known for her bravery and chameleonlike ability to blend in, whether she was masquerading as a black slave or "disguised" as a woman. She successfully fought for the Union as Frank Thompson until she became sick with malaria. She checked herself into a private hospital to avoid having to reveal her true identity. But when she learned that "Frank Thompson" was listed as a deserter, she came clean, and worked as a nurse for the Union—under her real name—until the end of the war. She wrote about her experiences in a memoir titled *Nurse and Spy in the Union Army*.

Rose O'Neal Greenhow spied so well for the Confederacy that Jefferson Davis credited her with winning the battle of Manassas. She was imprisoned twice, once in her own home, and the second time with her eight-year-old daughter in Washington, D.C.'s Old Capital Prison. After she was released from prison, she was exiled to the Confederate states, where Jefferson Davis enlisted her as a courier to Europe.

Nancy Hart served as a Confederate spy, carrying messages between the southern armies. When she was twenty, she was captured by the Union; she was able to escape after shooting one of her guards with his own weapon.

Elizabeth Van Lew was a spy for the North. She realized when she visited Union prisoners held by the Confederates in Richmond that they were excellent sources of information, as they had been marched through Confederate lines. Over the next four years, she worked as a spy, bringing food and clothing to Union prisoners and smuggling out information. For her efforts, she was made Postmaster of Richmond by General Grant.

Dr. Mary Edwards Walker was an abolitionist, a prisoner of war, a feminist, and a surgeon who dressed as a man and worked as a physician and spy for the Union. She is the only woman ever to receive the Congressional Medal of Honor.

Harriet Tubman is most famous for her work in freeing slaves, but she also served with the Union Army in South Carolina, organizing a spy network and leading expeditions in addition to fighting as a soldier, working as a cook and laundress, and aiding the wounded as a nurse. Through her experience with the Underground Railroad, leading more than 300 slaves to freedom, she came to know the landscape intimately and was able to recruit former slaves to be her eyes and ears, reporting on movements of the Confederate troops and scouting out the rebel camps. In 1863 she went on a gunboat raid, with Colonel James Montgomery and several black soldiers, that ultimately freed more than 700 slaves, thanks to the inside information from Harriet's scouts.

Ginnie and Lottie Moon were sisters who spied for the Confederates during the Civil War. Lottie began her career as a spy delivering messages for an underground Confederate organization at the behest of her husband. Ginnie too delivered messages over Union lines, on the pretext that she was meeting a beau. Ginnie and the girls' mother risked considerable danger when they accepted a mission to retrieve sensitive papers and supplies from the Knights of the Golden Circle in Ohio. They were apprehended by Union agents; Ginnie was able to swallow the most important written information they carried, but their cache of medical supplies was discovered and confiscated, and they were put under house arrest. Lottie came in disguise to plead with General Burnside—a former beau—for their release, but instead she was placed under arrest with her sister and mother. Ultimately the charges were dropped. Lottie eventually became a journalist, and in the 1920s Ginnie headed to Hollywood, where she had bit parts in several movies—none of them with plots as exciting as the sisters' real life adventures.

WORLD WAR I SPIES

Two famous and controversial World War I women spies, both of whom were executed, were Mata Hari (born Margaretha Geertruida Zelle McLeod) and Edith

Cavell. Mata Hari was a dancer who used her vocation as a cover for her spy work for the Germans. She was shot by the French as a spy in 1917. Edith Cavell was a British nurse who worked in Belgium during the war. She secretly helped British, French, and Belgian soldiers escape from behind the German lines, and she hid refugees in the nursing school she ran. By 1915 she had helped more than 200 British, French, and Belgian soldiers, but the Germans grew suspicious and arrested her. She was executed by firing squad.

WORLD WAR II SPIES

Virginia Hall, an American originally from Baltimore, Maryland, spied for the French during World War II. She was chased by the Nazis over the Pyrenees Mountains into Spain and eluded them, even though she had a wooden leg. After escaping, she trained as a radio operator and transferred to the OSS, America's secret spy agency. In 1943 she returned to France as an undercover spy, gathering intelligence, helping to coordinate air drops in support of D-Day, and working with the French underground to disrupt German communications. After the war, Virginia was awarded America's Distinguished

Service Cross, the only American civilian woman to receive such an honor. She continued to work for the OSS, and later the CIA, until her retirement in 1966.

Princess Noor-un-nisa Inayat Khan was an author and a heroine of the French Resistance. The Princess trained as a wireless operator in Great Britain and was sent into occupied France as a spy with the code name "Madeleine." She became the sole communications link between her unit of the French Resistance and home base before she was captured by the Gestapo and executed.

Violette Bushell Szabo was recruited and trained by the British Special Operations Executive after her husband, a member of the French Foreign Legion, was killed in North Africa. She was sent to France, where she was captured during a shoot-out. She refused to give up her information and was sent to the Ravensbruck concentration camp, where she was eventually killed. She was awarded the George Cross and the Croix de Guerre posthumously in 1946.

Amy Elizabeth Thorpe, also known as Betty Pack and "Code Name Cynthia," was an American spy first recruited by the British secret service and later by the American OSS. She is probably best remembered for her procurement of French naval codes, necessary to the Allies' invasion of North Africa, which she accomplished by tricking a man connected to the Vichy French Embassy into giving them to her. Not only did she steal French naval code books from the safe in his locked room, she also stole his heart: after the war they were married, and they spent the rest of their lives together.

❧

Spy Lingo

The word "spy" comes to us from various ancient words meaning "to look at or watch." And indeed, despite the modern movie emphasis on technology and machines as integral to a spy's bag of tricks, in essence what makes an excellent spy is her ability to watch, pay attention, look, and learn. But when a spy needs to communicate with other spies, code words and secret spy vocabulary are the tools that serve her best. Here are some of our favorite, top-secret spy words.

Agent   A person officially employed by an intelligence service (also: undercover agent, a secret agent; deep-cover agent, an agent under permanent cover; double agent, an agent simultaneously working for two enemies; Agent-in-Charge, the head agent)

Babysitter   Bodyguard

Blowback   Unexpected negative consequences of spying.

Blown	Detected, as in "your cover is blown."
Burn notice	An official statement from an intelligence agency stating that an individual or group is an unreliable source.
Chicken feed	Low-grade information fed through a double agent to an adversary with the intention of building the credibility of the double agent.
Cobbler	Spy who creates false passports, visas, diplomas and other documents.
Cover	A secret identity.
Dead drop	A secret hiding place somewhere in public where communications, documents, or equipment is placed for another agent to collect.
Ears only	Material too secret to commit to writing.

Eyes only   Documents that may be
read but not discussed.

Floater   A person used occasionally or even
unknowingly for an intelligence
operation.

Ghoul   Agent who searches obituaries and
graveyards for names of the deceased
for use by agents.

Informant	A person who provides intelligence to the surveillance team.
Joe	A deep-cover agent.
Mole	An agent who penetrates enemy organizations.
Peep	Photographer
Pocket Litter	Items in a spy's pocket (receipts, coins, theater tickets, etc.) that add authenticity to her identity.
Ring	A network of spies or agents.
Safehouse	A hideout unknown to the adversary.
Target	The person being spied on. (Also **Hard Target:** A target who actively maintains secrecy and may not reveal that she has detected the surveillance team.)

The Take	Information gathered by spying.
Trigger	An agent who watches for the target and alerts the rest of the surveillance team when the target is spotted.
Unsub	An unknown subject in a surveillance operation.
Undercover	Disguising your identity, or using an assumed identity, in order to learn secret information.
Wheel Artist	An outdoor surveillance specialist operating in a vehicle.

Layers of the Earth

The Earth is made up of several distinct layers: the relatively cool, thin outer crust; the warm, thick mantle; and the fiery hot and deep core.

CRUST

The Earth's outer shell consists of two parts: the oceanic crust and the continental crust. The continental crust (the ground, to you and me) is the second smallest area of the Earth and can be anywhere from 20 to 45 miles thick. This layer is mostly made up of granite, though it also contains silicon, aluminum, calcium, sodium and potassium.

The oceanic crust (or what we might think of as the bottom of the sea) is the smallest part of the Earth. It is between 3 and 6 miles thick, and most of the ocean floor is composed mostly of basalt (a type of rock) generated from volcanic activity. (Hawaii and Iceland are two island clusters that came into existence from accumulated basalt.) This thin, oceanic layer is also where new crust is formed.

The crust is divided into continental plates, which drift a few centimeters each year across the Earth's mantle.

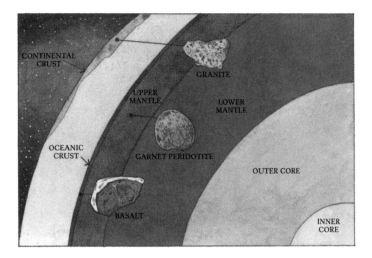

MANTLE

The Earth's mantle, at 1800 miles thick, is the largest inner layer. Like the crust, it also has two main sections: the upper mantle and the lower mantle. Together, the crust and the upper mantle are referred to as the lithosphere (from the Greek words "lithos," or rocky, and "sphaira," ball).

The upper mantle is rigid rock, including basaltic magma (molten rock) and garnet peridotite. Volcano excavations have shown that the mantle is made of crystalline forms of Olivine (a mineral, one of the most common ones on Earth) and pyroxene (a kind of rock-forming silicate mineral, which is a mineral containing silicon and oxygen). But it's not entirely solid: the part of the upper mantle called the asthenosphere (from the Greek "a," meaning without, plus "sthenos," strength; so, "without strength"), which is about 125 miles below the surface, is a weak, soft zone that seems to be molten and flexible rather than rigid like the rest of the upper mantle.

The lower mantle is made up of many chemicals, including silicon, magnesium, oxygen, iron, calcium, and aluminum. It is dense, very hot—temperatures towards the bottom of the mantle are as high as 6700° F—and fluid, flowing at a rate of a few centimeters per year.

CORE

Deep in the center of the Earth is the Earth's core. The molten, fluid outer core, which is roughly the size of Mars, is like electrically conductive hot lava. Its flowing motion and convection currents, combined with the Earth's rotation, is what creates the Earth's magnetic field. The inner core, about the size of the Moon and made out of pure iron, is under so much pressure that it is fused solid. The core is so hot that its temperature reaches about 10,000°F—hotter than even the surface of the Sun!

Layers of the Air

The word atmosphere (from the Greek "atmos," or breath, and "sphaira," ball) refers to the gas surrounding any planet or star. Earth's atmosphere, which is held close by Earth's gravity, is made up of nitrogen, oxygen, argon, carbon dioxide, trace amounts of other gases, and a small amount of water vapor—in other words, what we call "air." Our atmosphere provides a barrier from the sun's ultraviolet radiation and a cushion against the varying extremes of temperature from day to night.

Like the inner Earth, the outer Earth also has layers, distinct areas extending above it into the invisible air, that possess their own temperatures and effects.

TROPOSPHERE

Closest to the Earth, starting anywhere from just above the Earth's surface and extending as high as 60,000 feet up, is the Troposphere (from the Greek "tropos," meaning turning or change). Most of our weather systems are contained within the troposphere, which gets colder as it extends higher up. Eighty percent of the atmosphere's total mass is contained in this layer.

STRATOSPHERE

This layer, from the Latin "stratus" (to stretch or extend), stretches out to about 160,000 feet above the Earth and contains the ozone layer, which is about 50,000—115,000 feet above Earth's surface. The lower part of the stratosphere possesses a near-constant temperature, but this layer of atmosphere (unlike the troposphere) increases in heat as it gets higher. Commercial airplanes often fly in the lowest regions of the stratosphere to avoid the turbulence and bad weather encountered in the highest reaches of the troposphere.

MESOSPHERE

The mesosphere (from the Greek word "mesos," or middle) extends from about 160,000 feet to 285,000 feet and is the coldest of the atmospheric layers—colder even than the lowest temperature ever recorded in Antarctica (-129°F!). This

LAYERS OF THE AIR

freezing layer is helpful in protecting Earth from being hit by meteors: most meteors burn up when they enter this part of Earth's atmosphere. Not much is known about the mesosphere, due to the fact that it begins just slightly higher than the maximum altitude allowed for aircraft but lower than the minimum altitude for rocketships and other space craft. Due to these limitations, the atmospheric mesosphere has not been fully explored, leading some scientists to refer to it as the "ignorosphere."

THERMOSPHERE

Just above the mesosphere, the thermosphere extends from about 285,000 feet to over 400,000 feet. Named for the Greek "thermos," which means heat, this layer gets increasingly hotter as it extends farther away from the Earth. But even though it is so warm (temperatures can be as hot as 27,000° F!), it is so empty of matter that a normal thermometer would read the temperature as being way below zero. The thermosphere also contains the ionosphere, which is the part of the atmosphere ionized by solar radiation. It is also the area where auroras like the Aurora Borealis, or "Northern Lights," are formed.

EXOSPHERE

This uppermost region of the atmosphere extends more than 6,000 miles into space. At this level, the last level before outer space, only the lightest gases (mostly hydrogen, along with small amounts of helium, carbon dioxide, and atomic oxygen) are present. These density of these molecules are so low that there is barely any chance that they will collide with each other. With no collisions holding them back, they are able to escape the Earth's gravitational pull and drift into space. The exosphere is also where many satellites orbit the Earth.

∼

Basketball

Basketball was first played with a soccer ball and a suspended wooden peach basket when it was invented in 1891 by Dr. James Naismith at a YMCA in Springfield, Massachusetts. Girls originally shot hoops wearing Victorian petticoats, white muslin pinafores, and silk slippers. The dress code has thankfully changed, and basketball today is one of the few team sports that a girl can not only learn in elementary school but also dream of playing professionallly.

Basketball opened up to girls—real uniforms and all—in the 1970s. The United States passed a law known popularly as "Title IX" (the full name is Title IX of the Education Amendment of 1972), which said that no one, girls or boys, can be excluded from participating in school activities if that school receives federal funds. Some schools resisted, but many more decided to open up team sports to girls. As a result of Title IX, girls can now play sports at all school levels, and college women's basketball in particular has become a popular sport to watch and play.

Women's basketball made its Olympics premiere in

Shooting Guard

Point Guard

Small Forward

Power Forward

Center

1996, and the American team won the gold. In 1997, the Women's National Basketball Association launched with star players, including Sheryl Swopes, Rebecca Lobo, Lisa Leslie, and Cynthia Cooper. Of course, none of this matters if you're playing a pickup game or shooting solo at the hoop in front of the house.

WHO'S ON THE TEAM

Point Guard: She's the shortest, quickest, and best ball-handling player on the team. The Point Guard doesn't shoot much, but she is the team leader on the court and manages the plays.

Shooting Guard: She specializes in getting the ball in the basket and scoring points. She's skilled in hitting those three-point baskets from outside the line and darting to the basket for layups. Great with the ball, she can throw, dribble, and shoot in her sleep.

Center: She's the strongest, tallest, and highest-jumping player on the team. On college and professional teams, all eyes are on the Center. The Center rules the free-throw lane, and she shoots from right under the basket. She gets right into the mix, creates the space to shoot and score, and is also a major factor on defense for rebounding.

Power Forward: She grabs the rebounding ball from the other team's point, fast breaks it down the court, dribbles hard, and passes to the Center. She's also a good shooter. Actually, all the players need to be good shooters.

Small Forward: The Forward does it all. She shoots, runs, passes the ball, and scores, scores, scores. She's the ultimate player, and can substitute for anyone.

Of course, none of this matters if you're playing a pickup game or shooting solo at the hoop in front of the house.

Every Girl's Toolbox

When you know how to use tools, you can make stuff, and that is a powerful feeling. You can help your grandfather finish that dollhouse he's been tinkering with for years. You can make a swing for the backyard, a bench for your clubhouse—or make the whole clubhouse.

Experiment with wood, nails, screws, hammers, screwdrivers, and drills. After a while, you'll start to think in tools and materials, and you'll see how screws and nails hold wood together. Then you'll begin to come up with your own projects. Trial and error are the best teachers, and it doesn't take long to feel comfortable.

VISITING THE HARDWARE STORE

Before we turn to the basic tools, a word on hardware stores. You might be intimidated by them, as many people are. Especially those antiquated-looking, small hardware stores, with their dusty shelves filled to the brim with unfamiliar, scary-looking objects, usually guarded by men who are burly and possibly gruff.

Fear not, we are here to tell you. Said hardware stores mark the entrance to a world in which you can create and repair anything imaginable. And the hardware store's burly guardians? The truth is, they may look gruff, but usually they're very nice, and they love to problem-solve and to find the perfect nail or wire for you. Ask for help when you're matching bolts and nuts. Get their advice on what kind of drill bit will attach a wood plaque to the stone wall outside your house. They'll show you where to find hardware store exotica, and they know fix-it secrets you'll never learn in books.

Besides, many of them have daughters, too, and you can bet they've taught their girls a thing or two about what to do with a hammer and a box of nails.

CREATING YOUR TOOLBOX

Every girl needs her own toolbox. You can get a decent toolbox, with a latch and an organizing tray, for as little as ten dollars. Here are the basics to fill it with.

1. Safety Glasses

These are an absolute must when hammering, drilling, or sawing.

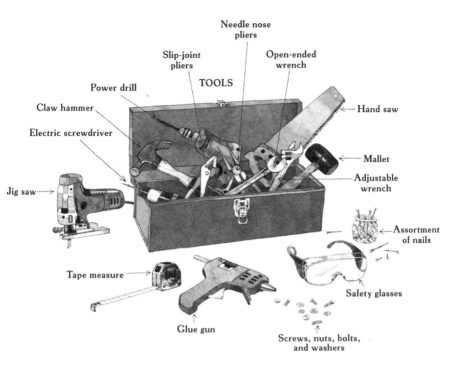

Needle nose pliers

Slip-joint pliers

Open-ended wrench

Power drill

TOOLS

Claw hammer

Electric screwdriver

Hand saw

Jig saw →

Mallet

Adjustable wrench

← Assortment of nails

Tape measure

Safety glasses

Glue gun

Screws, nuts, bolts, and washers

2. Claw Hammer

The flat side of the hammer bangs nails into wood; the V-shaped claw side pulls them out.

To hammer, grip the handle solidly, near the bottom. Hold a nail with your thumb and forefinger, and tap it in to the wood, gently, until it stands on its own. Then move your fingers away and hammer harder, from your forearm (that is, don't use your entire arm), and keep your wrist straight. Keep your eye on the nail, and trust your eye-hand coordination.

3. Nails

The measurements for nails derive from the British custom of selling 100 nails for a certain number of pennies. Nails are thus described in pennyweights, except the resulting abbreviation is not p, but, oddly enough, d, in reference to an ancient Roman coin, the denarius.

Once upon a time you could walk into a store in Yorkshire and purchase one hundred 1½-inch nails for 4 pence, and because of that, they are now labeled 4d nails. Much of the world, it must be said, uses the metric system for a more systematic and reasonable way to measure nails.

4. Screwdriver

The screwdriver not only gets screws where they're going and takes them out, it can be used in a bazillion creative ways to do almost anything. Try a 6-in-1 screwdriver (which has six changeable heads). To get jobs done faster, we recommend a battery-operated screwdriver.

5. Screws

Screws and bolts live in those mysteriously thin cabinets in the back aisle of the hardware store, along with their friends, bolts, nuts, and washers. Tighten a nut on a bolt to keep things ultra-secure. A washer—that's a flat circular object that slips on the bolt between the nut and the surface—protects the surface and helps tighten the nut.

Remembering the saying "righty-tighty, lefty-loosy" will help you recall which direction to turn a screw.

6. Wrench

Wrenches tighten and untighten the nuts that go at the end of bolts. They come in the open-end (fixed size) variety, and the adjustable. A small set of open-end wrenches, or one adjustable wrench, should start you off well.

7. Pliers

For gripping objects, like a stuck faucet, get a versatile groove-joint pliers. Also handy is a needle-nose pliers to grab small objects, like wire. It often has a little wire cutter built in (peek at the intersection of the handles and you'll find it).

8. Glue Gun

When you can't use screws, bolts, or nails, a glue gun saves the day, and is quite fun to operate. A small one should do, and don't forget plenty of glue sticks to melt in it.

9. Tape Measure

A 16-foot retractable tape measure that can lock in place is a good start.

10. Saw

A saw is not for the very young, of course, but it's a necessity for cutting wood to size and making shapes. A handsaw is a flat hand tool. A modern jigsaw is a power tool, activated by a trigger. All power tools are extremely dangerous if they are not used exactly as specified in their instructions, and you should always have adult supervision when operating them.

Hold long strips of wood on a sawhorse (a beam connected by four legs); cut small pieces of wood off the edge of a work table. Be careful, ask for help, and, as always, use your safety glasses.

11. Drill

To drill, start with an awl or center punch (hand tools that look like small spikes) to make an indentation in your surface so the drill bit won't slip. Bits are the small cutting pieces you fit into your drill for each project.

A battery-operated power drill is very handy. It will come with a basic set of bits, or you can get a set if it doesn't. There's an art to matching up the right drill bit to the size of the hole you'll need for the screw. If you know the size of the bolt or screw, that helps. Otherwise, the best we can tell you is to peer closely at the sizes and when in doubt try the smaller bit first. Experience will make it all the more clear.

Once you have your own toolbox, you might begin to truly love the hardware store. You'll stand for hours looking at the display of unique drill bits to make holes in metal, brick, plastic, or stone; at the sander attachment that can remove paint or brush wood's rough edges clean; at the buffer that smoothes it to perfection. You'll handle each one carefully, and after much deliberation with the burly hardware store guy about the pros and cons of each, take some home to try out on a project of your own imagination.

French Terms

NUMBERS

0	zéro	8	huit	16	seize
1	un	9	neuf	17	dix-sept
2	deux	10	dix	18	dix-huit
3	trois	11	onze	19	dix-neuf
4	quatre	12	douze	20	vingt
5	cinq	13	treize	100	cent
6	six	14	quatorze	1000	mille
7	sept	15	quinze	10,000	dix mille

FUN THINGS TO SAY

Mon frère
my brother (for sibling and friend)

Ouille ! Aïe !
(pronounced Oo-y! Ah-ee!) Ouch!

Ma soeur
my sister (for sibling and friend)

Zut ! Or Zut alors !
An expression of surprise (like "Darn it!")

Ben . . . euh
Well, er . . .

J'ai la pêche!
Literally "I've got the peach!" Full of energy and ready to go. (You can also say *J'ai la patate, J'ai la banane, J'ai la frite*—I've got the potato, I've got the banana, I've got the fries!)

Une soirée pyjama
A pajama party

TONGUE TWISTERS *(Les Virelangues)*

Les chaussettes de l'archiduchesse sont-elles sèches? Archi-sèches!
"The archduchess's socks are dry, extra dry!"

Un chasseur sachant chasser doit savoir chasser sans son chien.
"A hunter knowing how to hunt has to know how to hunt without his [hunting] dog."

Si ces six-cent saucissons-ci sont six-cent sous,
ces six-cent-six saucissons-là sont six-cent-six sous.
"If these 600 salami cost 600 pennies, those 606 salamis cost 606 pennies."

Je veux et j'exige d'exquises excuses.
"I want and I demand delightful apologies."

FOOD

Frites
French fries

Pâtes au gruyère
Macaroni and cheese

Crème au chocolat
Chocolate pudding

Flan au caramel
Caramel custard

Yaourths à boire
Drinkable yogurt

Fondant au chocolat
Small chocolate cakes with
warm, melting insides

Tarte sablée au citron
Lemon pie with a tender,
buttery crust

TRAVEL AND ADVENTURE

Où est la gare routière?
Where is the central bus station?

Quand part le prochain bateau pour Tunis et combien coûte le voyage?
When is the next boat to Tunis, and how much does the fare cost?

Devons nous visiter le Comoros pour voir le volcan du Mont Karthala?
Shall we visit the Comoros to see the volcano at Mount Karthala?

࿏

French Around the World

Bien sur (of course!), French is the primary language of France. But did you know that it is also an official language of more than fifty-five francophone nations and regions around the globe? Among these are the Democratic Republic of the Congo, Canada, Madagascar, Côte d'Ivoire, Cameroon, Burkina Faso, Niger, Senegal, Mali, Belgium, Chad, Guinea, Rwanda, Haiti, Burundi, Benin, Switzerland, Togo, Central African Republic, Lebanon, Republic of the Congo, Gabon, Comoros, Equatorial Guinea, Djibouti, Luxembourg, Vanuatu, Seychelles, Monaco, and more.

Fun Fact: With over one billion speakers, the most-spoken language on earth is Mandarin Chinese. The list of other top-spoken world languages also includes English; Hindi-Urdu and the other languages of India; Spanish; Russian; Arabic; Bengali; Portuguese; the Malay languages of Indonesia; and French.

∼⌒

French is spoken in the Arabic-speaking North African

countries of Morocco, Algeria, Tunisia, and Mauritania, a reflection of their former status as French-occupied colonies. In Senegal, another former colony, French is spoken alongside native languages like Wolof, Pulaar, Jola, and Mandinka.

Fun Fact: North Africa is sometimes called the Maghreb, which in Arabic means the place of sunset, or "the west." The Maghreb is divided from the rest of Africa by the Atlas Mountains and by the Sahara desert.

～

Although the majority of Canada is English-speaking, the province of Québec is francophone, and it protects its French heritage fiercely. The capital is Québec City, and it was settled by French explorers and soldiers and fur traders in 1608, making it one of North America's oldest cities. The name sounds French, but it actually comes from an Algonquin word, "kebec," which means "where the river narrows."

Fun Fact: Québec City was originally named Stadacona by the native Wendat people who lived there.

Cajun French is still spoken in Louisiana. In the 1680's, the French explorer René-Robert de la Salle sailed southward down the Mississippi River. He named the region "Louisiana" after the powerful French king Louis XIV. French-speaking settlers arrived soon after from Acadia, which is the area around Nova Scotia, and they brought French with them. (You can see the connection to Cajun in how close the two words are. The settlers spoke "Acadian," which is easily morphed into "Cajun" by dropping the "A" and pronouncing the "d" as a "j"). Sometimes Cajun is confused with Creole, another Louisiana lan-

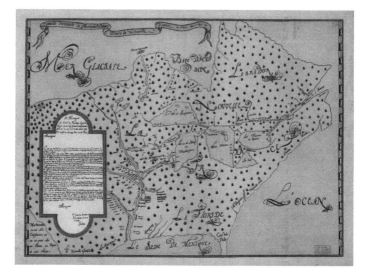

guage, which is a mixture of native, African, Caribbean, and Western-European language.

Fun Fact: De la Salle's ship *La Belle* sunk in Matagorda Bay, off the coast of Texas, and was discovered by archaeologists in 1995.

～○

Few people know that in Wisconsin there's a French-Belgian dialect called Walloon. In the 19th century, people left Wallonia, the French-speaking part of Belgium south of Brussels, and settled on the Wisconsin peninsula that sits between Green Bay and Lake Michigan. They brought the French-Belgian dialect of Walloon with them, and even today in Wisconsin, as in southern Belgium, you can hear phrases like *Bondjoû* (Hello), *Arvey* (Goodbye), and *Cmint daloz?* (How are you?).

ಾ

Joan of Arc

One life is all we have and we live it as we believe in living it. But to sacrifice what you are and to live without belief, that is a fate more terrible than dying. —Joan of Arc

Joan was born around 1412 in the small town of Domrémy in France, on the border of the provinces of Champagne and Lorraine, to Jacques d'Arc and Isabelle Romée. She grew up helping her father and brothers work the land and helping her mother, a devout woman, tend the house.

The year she turned twelve, she became convinced that there was something special about her—a destiny she alone could fulfill. She began hearing the voices of St. Michael, St. Catherine, and St. Margaret, whom she believed had been sent by God to inform her of her divine mission to save France. So compelled was she by the urgency of these voices that by the time she was fifteen she cut her hair, began dressing in a man's uniform, and took up arms.

France and England were deep into the Hundred Years' War at this point. At that time in history, the two

nations were not as separate as they are now, and there was a battle raging over who should be king of the general area. By 1429, Henry VI of England was claiming the throne and the English occupied Paris and all of northern France. Joan had two missions, thanks to the voices that guided her: to recover her homeland from English domination and reclaim the besieged city of Orleans; and to see the dauphin of France, Charles VII, crowned king. She left her home, without telling her parents, and appealed to the captain of the dauphin's army, telling him of her divine mission. He initially dismissed the notion of a fifteen-year-old girl having the leadership capacity to head his forces. However, her persistence and clarity of vision ultimately convinced him, and she went on to convince the dauphin as well that she was on a mission from God meant to save him and restore France. After being examined by a board of theologians, she was given the rank of captain and allowed to lead men into battle.

She was seventeen when she led her troops to victory over the English at the battle of Orleans in May 1429. She rode in white armor and carried a banner bearing the likenesses of her three saints. It wasn't all that unusual at that time for women to fight alongside men; indeed, throughout the Middle Ages women had, when necessary, worn armor, led armies, ridden horses, and defended castles and lands. Joan was an excellent leader. Through her self-assured confidence, her courage, and her determination, she was able to effectively command soldiers and captains alike. She organized her army of men into professional soldiers, and even required them to attend mass and go to confession. So formidable was her leadership that it was said when her troops approached, the enemy fled the battlefield. But by far her most innovative act was instilling among her people a sense of nationalism and patriotic pride: she was one of the first leaders to consider England and France as separate countries, with separate cultures and traditions that were worth fighting to preserve.

Due in great part to Joan's leadership on the battlefield, Charles VII was crowned king of France on July 17, 1429 in Reims Cathedral. Her victory, however, was short-lived: she was captured by the Burgundians in 1430 while defending Compiegne, near Paris, and was sold to the English. The English turned her over to the court at Rouen to be tried for witchcraft and crimes against the church. Though the witchcraft charge was dismissed (on the grounds that she was a virgin), she was accused of perpetrating crimes against God by wearing men's clothing. After a fourteen-month trial, during which she never strayed from her insistence on the divinity of her voices and the absolute rightness of her calling, Joan was convicted and burned at the stake in the Rouen marketplace on May 30, 1431. Her last words were, "Jesus! Jesus!" She was nineteen years old.

Almost twenty-five years after her death, Pope Callixtus III reopened the case at the request of Inquisitor-General Jean Brehal and Joan's mother Isabelle Romée. Joan was vindicated as a martyr and declared an innocent woman on July 7, 1456. It was nearly 500 years after her death that she was canonized as a saint, on May 16, 1920, by Pope Benedict XV. Joan of Arc is now recognized as the patron saint of France.

The story of a girl guided by voices to change the world has proved irresistible to storytellers and artists from the time of her death to the present day. She continues to serve as an inspiration to daring girls everywhere.

☙

The History of Writing, and Writing in Cursive Italics

The first writing instrument resembled the first hunting instrument: a sharpened stone. These stones were used to etch pictures on cave walls depicting visual records of daily life. Over time, drawings evolved into symbols that ultimately came to represent words and sentences, and the medium itself shifted from cave walls to clay tablets. Still, it wasn't until much later that the alphabet emerged to replace pictographs and symbols. Another milestone in the history of writing was the advent of paper in ancient China. The Greek scholar Cadmus, who was the founder of the city of Thebes and proponent of the Phoenician alphabet, was also the purported inventor of the original text message—letters, written by hand, on paper, sent from one person to another.

Some cultures lasted for many years before having a written language. In fact, Vietnamese wasn't written down until the 1600s. Two Portuguese Jesuit missionaries named Gaspar d'Amiral and Antonio Barboza Romanized the language by developing a writing and spelling system using the Roman alphabet and several signs to represent the tonal accents of Vietnamese speech. This system was further codified in the first comprehensive Vietnamese dictionary (containing over 8,000 words) by Frenchman Alexandre de Rhodes in 1651. This is why its written language uses Roman letters instead of characters like the surrounding Asian countries do.

At first, all letter-based writing systems used only uppercase letters. Once the writing instruments themselves became more refined, lowercase letters became possible. And as writing instruments improved, and the alphabet became more elaborate, handwriting became an issue. Today we have an incredible variety of things to write with—all manner of pens, pencils, markers, crayons—but the writing instrument most used in recent history was the quill pen, made from a bird feather.

Before we can discuss the art of writing with a quill pen, we must talk about penmanship. Even in the age of computers a clear handwriting style is a useful and necessary skill, and drawing a row of tall and loopy As or Ps or quirky-looking Qs, twenty to a line, and making them all look font-perfect, can actually be a pleasurable act. Nowadays, when we are more likely to type than to write with a pen, cursive might seem old-fashioned. But at the time of its invention, the notion of standardized handwriting was a revolutionary idea.

The first use of cursive writing, or Italian "running hand," was by Aldus Manutius, a fifteenth-century printer from Venice, whose name lives on today in the serif typeface "Aldus." Cursive simply means "joined together" (the word has its roots in the Latin verb *currere,* to run), and one of the primary benefits of the "running hand" was that it enabled the writer to write quickly, and took up less space. But the uniform look of the script proved equally useful: in later centuries, before the typewriter was invented, all professional correspondence was written in cursive, and employees—men—were trained to write in "a fair hand," so that all correspondence appeared in the exact same script. (Women were taught to write in a domestic, looping script.)

With the introduction of computers and standardized fonts, handwriting cursive documents is no longer seen

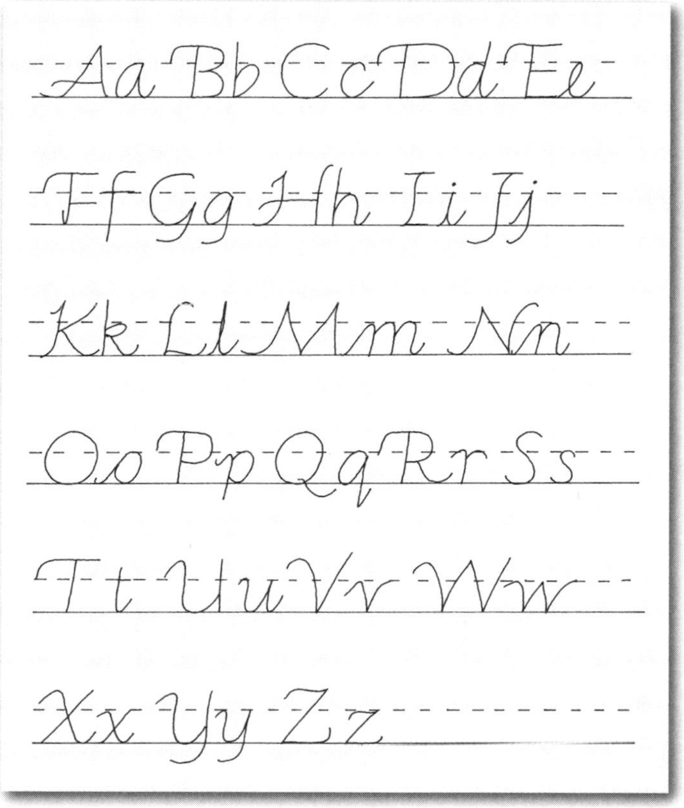

Aa Bb Cc Dd Ee

Ff Gg Hh Ii Jj

Kk Ll Mm Nn

Oo Pp Qq Rr Ss

Tt Uu Vv Ww

Xx Yy Zz

Cursive Italic

I am a daring girl

as professional business etiquette—although for invitations, certificates, and greeting cards, hand-written is still the sophisticated way to go.

Nowadays, there are several schools of thought about what nice cursive writing looks like, and writing in "a fair hand" is no longer entirely the province of men, as it originally was. Currently schoolchildren study a range of cursive, including D'Nealian, Getty-Dubay, Zaner-Bloser, Modern Cursive, Palmer, and Handwriting Without Tears. All of these styles are based on similar precepts about letter width and height, and all are designed to bring some uniformity and legibility to the handwritten word. (The Getty-Dubay team even has a series of seminars specially designed for the sloppiest of handwriters—doctors.)

Cursive Italic is a fancier way of writing cursive that can dress up even the most mundane correspondence. Like regular cursive, the letters are connected, but Cursive Italic has a more decided slant, and the rounded lowercase letters have more of a triangular shape to them. The form also lends itself to decorative flourishes, which is why you often see Cursive Italic used for wedding invitations, menus at fancy restaurants, and the like.

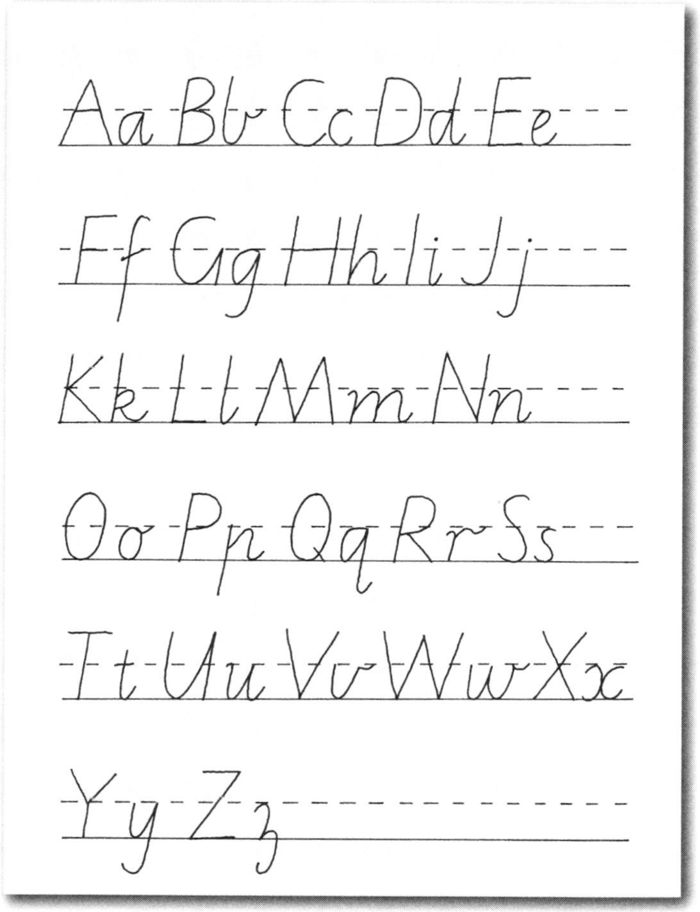

Aa Bb Cc Dd Ee

Ff Gg Hh Ii Jj

Kk Ll Mm Nn

Oo Pp Qq Rr Ss

Tt Uu Vv Ww Xx

Yy Zz

Victoria Modern Cursive

Adventure is worthwhile in itself.

Italic lettering is written at a slant of about 10° from the vertical, with your pen held at about a 45° angle from the baseline.

In Victoria, Australia, a new style of handwriting was developed in the mid-1980s for primary schools. Now Victoria Modern Cursive is used across the country and is appreciated for its readability as well as its ease of elaboration—a few flourishes and the script is transformed from practical to fancy.

To practice, some writers like to write out their favorite poem as they work on perfecting their form. Here is a famous haiku from the eighteenth-century Japanese poet Issa that is a nice reminder of both the gradual evolution of human writing and the sometimes painstaking pace good penmanship requires.

Little snail
Inch by inch, climb
Mount Fuji!

A Short History of Women Inventors and Scientists

E ven though it's said that "necessity is the mother of invention," women's contributions to inventing and science have been, in the past, often overlooked. It's likely women have been using their creativity and intelligence to engineer new ideas and products since the beginning of human experience, but nobody really kept track of such things until a few hundred years ago. Below we've assembled some of our favorite daring women inventors, scientists, and doctors—from Nobel Prize winners to crafters of practical devices, from women who revolutionized the way diapers were changed to women whose revolutionary ideas changed the world.

A SHORT HISTORY OF WOMEN INVENTORS AND SCIENTISTS

1715

Sybilla Masters becomes the first American woman inventor in recorded history, though in accordance with the laws of the time, her patent for "Cleansing Curing and Refining of Indian Corn Growing in the Plantations" was issued in her husband Thomas' name by the British courts.

1809

Mary Dixon Kies of Connecticut becomes the first U.S. woman to be issued a patent in her own name, for her invention of a process for weaving straw with silk or thread.

1870

Martha Knight becomes the first woman in the United States to fight and win a patent suit, when she defends her patent against a man who had stolen her design for a machine that produced flat-bottomed bags and filed for his own patent on it. He said a woman couldn't possibly have the mechanical knowledge needed to invent such a complex machine, but Knight was able to back up her claim.

1885

Sarah E. Goode, born a slave in 1850, obtains the first patent by an African American woman inventor for her folding cabinet bed, a space-saver that when folded up could be used as a desk, complete with compartments for stationery and writing supplies.

1902

Ida Henrietta Hyde is named the first female member of the American Physiological Society. She was also the first woman to graduate from the University of Heidelberg and the first woman to do research at the Harvard Medical School. She went on to invent the microelectrode in the 1930s.

1903

Scientist **Marie Curie** is awarded the Nobel Prize in Physics for her discovery of the radioactive elements radium and polonium. She is awarded the Nobel Prize again in 1911 (this time in Chemistry), making her the first person to win two Nobel prizes.

1914

Mary Phelps Jacob invents the modern bra after becoming fed up with restrictive corsets. Her brassiere, made from two silk handkerchiefs and a ribbon, became so popular that after she patented the invention, she went on to sell it to the Warner Corset Company.

1932

Hattie Elizabeth Alexander, an American pediatrician and microbiologist, develops a serum to combat Hemophilus influenzae, which at the time has a fatality rate of 100 percent in infants. In 1964, she becomes the first woman to be elected president of the American Pediatric Society.

1935

Irene Joliot Curie, the daughter of Marie Curie, is awarded the Nobel Prize for Chemistry with her husband, for their discovery of radioactivity, making the Curies the family with most Nobel laureates to date.

1941

The actress **Hedy Lamarr** invents (along with George

Anthiel) a "Secret Communications System" to help combat the Nazis in World War II.

1950

Marion Donovan invents the disposable diaper. She sells her company along with her diaper patents to Keko Corporation in 1951 for one million dollars.

1951

Bessie Nesmith invents Liquid Paper, a quick-drying white liquid painted onto paper to correct mistakes.

1952

Mathematician and U.S. naval officer Rear Admiral **Grace Murray Hopper** invents the computer compiler and helps to develop the first user-friendly business computer programming language, COBOL (COmmon Business-Oriented Language).

1953

Dr. Virginia Apgar, a professor of anesthesiology at the New York Columbia-Presbyterian Medical Center, devises the Apgar Scale, a test now used all over the world to determine the physical status of a newborn baby.

1957

Rachel Fuller Brown and **Elizabeth Lee Hazen,** researchers for the New York Department of Health, develop the anti-fungal antibiotic drug nystatin. They were inducted into the National Inventors Hall of Fame in 1994.

1964

Chemist **Stephanie Louise Kwolek** invents Kevlar, a polymer fiber that is five times stronger than the same weight of steel and is now used in bulletproof vests, helmets, trampolines, tennis rackets, tires, and many other common objects.

1966

Physicist **Lillian Gilbreth** becomes the first woman to be elected to the National Academy of Engineering.

1975

Physicist **Betsy Ancker-Johnson** becomes the fourth woman elected to the National Academy of Engineering, one of the highest honors an engineer can receive.

1975

Nuclear Physicist **Dr. Chien-Shiung Wu** is elected the first woman president of the American Physical Society.

1983

Barbara McClintock, an American scientist and cyto-geneticist, becomes the first woman to win, unshared, the Nobel Prize in Physiology or Medicine, for her discovery of a genetic mechanism called transposition.

1988

Biochemist **Gertrude Belle Elion** is awarded the Nobel Prize in Physiology or Medicine.

1991

Chemist **Edith Flanigen** is the first woman to be awarded the Perkin Medal, the nation's most distinguished honor in applied chemistry.

1993

Ellen Ochoa, an electrical engineer who holds many patents on high-tech optical recognition systems, becomes the first Hispanic female astronaut in space.

1995

Physical chemist **Isabella Helen Lugoski Karle** receives the National Medal of Science for her work on the structure of molecules.

1997

Dr. Rosalyn Sussman Yalow wins the Nobel Prize in Medicine for her 1959 invention of RIA, a revolutionary way to diagnose illness at the molecular level.

1999

Eye surgeon **Dr. Patricia Bath** becomes the first African American woman doctor to receive a patent for a medical invention.

☙

Patent Facts

❖ The U.S. Patent Act of 1790 allowed anyone to protect his or her invention with a patent. However, because in many states women could not legally own property independent of their husbands, many women inventors didn't apply for patents, or only did so under their husbands' names.

❖ The majority of the U.S. origin patents held by women inventors are in chemical technologies.

❖ About 35 percent of the women granted U.S. patents between 1977 and 1996 were from California, New York, or New Jersey.

❖ With over 125 patents in areas related to organic compounds and textile processing, Dr. Giuliana Tesoro (born in 1921) is one of the most prolific scientists in the world.

The Fibonacci Sequence

The mysterious Fibonacci Sequence follows a deceptively simple plan. It begins with the numbers zero and one, and thereafter each number is the sum of the two numbers before it. The sequence looks like this:

0, 1, 1, 2, 3, 5, 8, 13, 21, 34, 55, 89, 144, 233, 377, 610, 987, and so forth.

And this is how it is made:

$$0 + 1 = 1,$$
$$1 + 1 = 2,$$
$$2 + 3 = 5$$
$$. . .$$
$$34 + 55 = 89,$$
$$55 + 89 = 144,$$
$$89 + 144 = 233, \text{ and so forth.}$$

RABBITS

The Fibonacci sequence originated from an arcane question about rabbits—namely: How many rabbits would be born each month to a single male-and-female pair of rabbits, if (after the first two months, in which baby rabbits are still bunnies and cannot yet give birth), each month the original pair and every other new rabbit pair give birth to a new pair of rabbits?

The Fibonacci sequence of numbers was to yield the answer, even though it didn't account for the fact that some rabbits might give birth to more than two bunnies, some bunnies might die, and others might not reproduce.

But no matter. If the sequence failed to predict the real-world habits of bunnies and rabbits, it did turn out to be an intriguingly powerful set of numbers. Each number in the Fibonacci sequence, it was quickly discovered, when divided by the number directly before it, equals approximately 1.61803. The ratio became especially accurate as the numbers in the sequence got larger and larger. For instance, 8 divided by 5 equals 1.6, and 55 divided by 34 equals 1.617647058. By the time the sequence reaches 610, the number appears exactly: 610 divided by 377 is 1.61803, and 1597 divided by 987 equals 1.61803.

THE GOLDEN RATIO

PHI

The discovery was startling because 1.61803 is the classic Golden Ratio. Also called Phi—after the sculptor Phidias, who lived during the Greek Golden Age of the fifth century, B.C.—the Golden Ratio shows up across the arts, in the architecture of buildings, in musical pitches, and in the rhythm of poetry. The width and length of the ancient Parthenon, built in Phidias' time, followed the Golden Ratio, too, because Greek builders considered a rectangle with the sides in the ratio of 1: 1.61803 to be most pleasing to the eye. The painter Leonardo DaVinci called the ratio the Divine Proportion. He believed it was the ultimate key to beauty and harmony, and he used it to construct the proportions of the famous Mona Lisa's face.

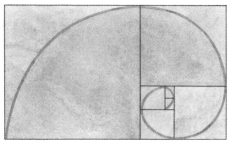

Fibonacci rectangle with Golden Spiral

The Golden Ratio appears throughout the natural world, too: in the center of a daisy, a sunflower's petals, and the whorl of a pinecone's scales. The spiral of a nautilus shell maps directly onto a Fibonacci rectangle. The shell's shape is an arc that becomes visible when opposing corners of the squares of a Fibonacci rectangle are connected. Because of this, the nautilus shell has been called the Golden Spiral.

The Golden Ratio of 1: 1.61803 can also be measured on the human body. The length from the belly-button to the floor and the measure of the top of the head to the floor is a Golden Ratio, and so is the relationship of the length of the hand to the combined measure of the hand and the forearm.

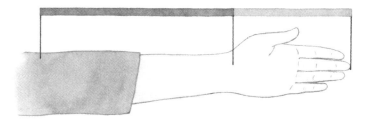

THE FIBONACCI RECTANGLE
IS MADE LIKE THIS:

♦ Begin by drawing one small square.

♦ Next to it, draw the same size square. The two squares form a rectangle.

♦ Draw the next square using the measured length of the first rectangle's longer side; this makes the new square the sum of the two before it, as the Fibonacci sequence demands.

♦ Continue to draw each new square using the measure of the longer side of each prior rectangle.

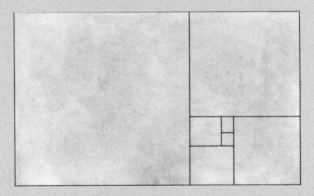

LEONARDO FIBONACCI

The Fibonacci sequence got its name from a medieval Italian mathematician named Leonardo of Pisa. Leonardo's father was a businessman and trader. When Leonardo was young, their family lived for many years in North Africa, in the Algerian port city now called Béjaïa. Leonardo accompanied his father to ports of call throughout the Mediterranean, from Sicily and Cyprus all the way to Syria. Some people nicknamed Leonardo "Fibonacci" because he was the son—*Filius,* shortened to *Fi*—of the man named Bonacci; hence, Fibonacci. Others called him Leonardo Bigollo, which means Leonard the traveler.

In Fibonacci's time, Europeans did math with Roman numerals. That's the system he was taught as a young schoolboy in Italy. The problem is, with Roman numerals there is no way to perform math operations beyond simple addition and subtraction. The Roman system doesn't even have a zero. When his family moved to North Africa, Fibonacci learned a very different way to count, with the Hindu-Arabic numerals still in use today, and he learned to work with decimal points and place value columns.

Intrigued by the differences between the two systems, Fibonacci wrote a book—in Latin, so that European scholars could read it—called *Liber Abaci,* which was published in the early 1200s. He described the Hindu-Arabic numerals, and he wrote instructions learned from mathematicians in India about how to add, subtract, multiply, and divide. This was common knowledge in the Arabic-speaking world that stretched from North Africa to the borders of India. But this math was dramatically new for Europe, and it changed the course of European history. Mathematicians and scholars saw the great potential in the new number and math system, and Fibonacci became a celebrity.

ROMAN NUMERALS	I	II	III	IV	V	VI	VII	VIII	IX	X
ARABIC NUMERALS	1	2	3	4	5	6	7	8	9	10

There's one final twist to the story. The sequence we know as Fibonacci's was not actually discovered by Fibonacci. It was known in India as the Hemachandra numbers, named after Acharya Hemachandra, a Jain monk who was also a mathematician, a poet, and a scholar, and who lived from 1089 to 1173. It seems that it was Hemachandra, and not Fibonacci, who first discovered the number sequence, as part of his quest to understand the cadences of Indian poetry.

Queens of the Ancient World: Boudica

Boudica was a warrior queen, with a fierce way about her and brilliant red hair that flowed to her waist. As Queen of the Celtic tribe of the Iceni in the first century AD, Boudica organized a revolt against the Romans, hoping to regain and protect her people's independence.

In the year 43 AD, Roman soldiers marched to the French edge of the European continent, crossed the British Channel, and began their invasion of Britain. The Emperor Claudius, whose reign had begun in 41 and would last until 54, dreamed of conquering the mysterious British island. Rome was at the height of its power. Its huge army helped expand the boundaries of Rome in all directions. Britain was a special challenge. It sat beyond a choppy channel of water and was the farthest spot to the northwest that the Romans could imagine, with a cold, unfathomable, and terrifyingly large sea beyond.

Britain was the home of Celtic tribes and Druids, with their mystical traditions and religious groves of trees. In Rome, the lives of women and girls were as controlled as the tightly wound hair braids and coils that were the

fashion of the day. There, men dominated public life, and women, especially those in wealthy and powerful families, lived more private lives. By contrast, Celtic women had many more rights. They could govern and make laws, marry more freely, own property, and, alongside men, they could work and take part in their community's marketplace. Their hair, too, showed their freedom: the fashion was to grow it long and leave it down, ready to fly with the wind.

Boudica was of the Iceni tribe, which inhabited the eastern part of Britain, and she had married Prasutagus, the tribe's King. As Roman legions invaded and took over the land of the Celts, Boudica watched, unbelievingly. The Romans declared much of Britain to be the

Roman province of Britannia. They founded the cities of Londinium—now called London—and Camulodunum, which they made into their capital. There they built a massive Roman-style Temple to the Emperor Claudius and a towering statue of a woman representing Victory.

Facing troops with greater weapons, the Iceni and nearby Celtic tribes followed the path of many local tribes. They feared that active resistance would mean death for many and slavery for the rest, and so they submitted. When the Romans came to the Iceni kingdom, they decided that Prasutagus should continue to rule his people. The Iceni could remain semi-independent so long as they stayed loyal to Rome. The Romans often made arrangements like this, charging local rulers to keep the peace and to collect taxes for the Empire. Prasutagus' small kingdom lasted this way for nearly twenty years, until he died in the year 60, leaving behind Boudica and their two daughters.

Most of what we know about Boudica's life comes to us from the Roman historian Tacitus, who in 109 AD wrote the *Annals,* detailing Rome's first century exploits. Tacitus reports that under Roman rule, Prasutagus and Boudica remained prosperous. After Prasutagus' death, however, it was learned that he had been wheeling and dealing with the Romans, and this included borrowing a great deal of money from the Roman governor. Prasutagus' will directed that half the kingdom be turned over to the Romans to pay his debt. The other half he gave to his two daughters, for them to rule as queens.

Prasutagus had hoped his deathbed directions would protect his family, but this didn't happen. The Roman governor Suetonius had already decided that when Prasutagus died, he would disarm the Iceni people, confiscate their arrows and spears and darts, and annex their land fully into the Roman province of Britannia.

Roman soldiers soon arrived at Boudica's palace to plunder Prasutagus's wealth and claim his entire kingdom as their own. They captured Boudica and made a show of torturing her and her two daughters in front of the Iceni tribesmen and women. Their cousins, aunts, and uncles were made into slaves.

Later that year, the Roman governor Suetonius decided to conquer Wales, on Britain's western shore. As the soldiers of his fearsome Legion marched westward, they left the cities of Camulodunum and Londinium largely undefended.

Boudica sensed her chance. She claimed the mantle of leadership and stirred her people to reclaim their freedom and liberty. She reminded them of the horror and cruelty of Roman rule, and rallied them to win back their lands.

Boudica outlined her plan. Suetonius was in Wales, routing Druids on the Isle of Mona. Leading the way in her horse-drawn chariot, with 100,000 British fighters behind her, she would attack Camulodunum first. All around, miraculous omens pointed to Boudica's success; ancient reports tell us that the city's Victory statue fell from its tall base to the ground below with no cause, as if Rome were already yielding.

Boudica's troops stormed the city's gates. By day's end the city was in flames. A small group of Roman soldiers and leaders locked themselves inside the Temple of Claudius, holding out for two days until Boudica burned the Temple to the ground.

After hearing of Boudica's victory at Camulodunum, the Roman governor Suetonius left Wales and headed straight back to London to protect it from Boudica's rampaging soldiers. Seeing Boudica's willingness to burn cities to the ground, he decided, however, to abandon London to her fires. Boudica's soldiers left 25,000 people dead in London before advancing to Verulamium, Britain's third-largest city, where they killed everyone who had cooperated with the Romans, and then destroyed the city.

Boudica's army began to falter. As Suetonius' men approached, they burnt the crops in the fields, sending ripened corn and beans into smoke, and leaving nothing to feed Boudica's troops and keep them strong. Boudica had successfully destroyed unarmed cities, but Suetonius and his professional legions were too strong for the relatively untrained British Celts, whose luck now turned. Boudica fought one final battle, the place of which is unknown. Her troops had to start from the bottom of a tall hill and face off against the Romans, who were strategically encamped at the top. Roman arrows and pikes rained down on the Celts. Boudica's fighters were overpowered, and many were lost to battle.

The rebellion was over. As night fell, Boudica abandoned the glorious bronze chariot that had served her well. She grabbed her two teenage daughters by the hand and together the three of them ran through the darkness, returning home to their palace along hidden paths and back roads. Once home, they knew they would be captured and brought to Rome to be displayed in chains to the jeering crowds at the Coliseum. Instead, Boudica decided to end her own life by drinking a cup of poison, and her princess-daughters took the same route. It is said that when her closest relatives entered the palace, they found Boudica wearing her legendary tunic of brilliant colors, covered with a deep auburn cloak, her flaming red hair still untamed.

Words to Impress

Strunk and White, in *The Elements of Style,* tell us about sesquepedalian words: "Do not be tempted by a twenty-dollar word when there is a ten-center handy, ready, and able." But daring girls are never afraid to drop a spectacular multisyllabic bombshell when necessary. Here are some you can use when quotidian vocabulary fails.

brobdingnagian (brob-ding-NAG-ee-uhn)
gigantic, enormous, tremendous
Lydia made constant use of her brobdingnagian vocabulary.

crepuscular (kri-PUHS-kyuh-ler)
dim; resembling or having to do with twilight
Janet's habit of planning all her best pranks to occur immediately after dinner led her mother to declare her utterly crepuscular in nature.

diaphanous (dahy-AF-uh-nuhs)
almost entirely transparent or translucent
Halloween had been a success, thought Belinda, even though little kids kept bumping into her costume's diaphanous fairy wings.

gustatory (GUHS-tuh-tohr-ee)
of or pertaining to taste or tasting
Rachael dug into her dinner with gustatory glee.

ineluctable (in-ih-LUCK-tuh-bull)
inevitable, inescapable
(From the Latin word *luctari*, "to wrestle.")
Sarah was unable to escape the ineluctable gaze of her mother.

jejune (ji-JOON)
immature, uninteresting, dull; lacking nutrition
Molly resolved to use an interesting vocabulary, the better to avoid appearing jejune.

languorous (LANG-ger-uhs)
lacking spirit or liveliness; dreamy; lazy
Amelia spent a languorous day by the pool.

nemesis (NEM-uh-sis)

a source of harm; an opponent that cannot be beaten;
mythological Greek goddess of vengeance
On a good day, Christina's brother was her ally; on a
bad day, he was her nemesis.

persiflage (PURR-suh-flahzh)

light banter; frivolous discussion
"We must be careful to keep our persiflage to a minimum,"
Nola whispered to Margot during class.

quiescence (kwee-ES-uhns)

stillness, quietness, inactivity
Esme reveled in the extraordinary quiescence of early
morning when she awoke before anyone else.

rapprochement (rap-rohsh-MAHN)

reconciliation; the reestablishing of cordial relations
After holding a grudge against him for so long, Eleanor
felt it was almost a relief to have reached a rapproche-
ment with her brother.

truculent (TRUCK-yuh-lunt)
pugnacious, belligerent, scathing
When Nancy was pushed too far, she became truculent.

vitiate (VISH-ee-ayt)
to weaken, impair, or render invalid
Penelope's debate in class vitiated Rob's argument.
xenophobe (ZEE-nuh-fohb)
a person who fears or hates foreigners
*It was a nerve-racking moment at the potluck picnic, when
the neighborhood xenophobe showed up with potato salad.*

zeitgeist (TSIYT-giyst)
the spirit of the time; the outlook of a particular
generation
*Shonda was convinced the latest pop star embodied the
zeitgeist of middle school.*

॰

Softball

Softball was invented on Thanksgiving Day in 1887, in Chicago. Tales report that the first softball game was played indoors one winter, and that it made good use of a boxing glove and a stick. Did George Hancock, an enthusiastic reporter for the Chicago Board of Trade, really draw some white lines on the floor of the gym and shout "Let's play ball!" thus inaugurating softball? We'll never know for sure, but he did become intrigued by the new batting game with the large ball, and loved playing indoors while the snow fell and the chilly Chicago winter wind blew through the fields. By the turn of the twentieth century, softball had moved outdoors, and into summertime.

Everyone plays softball, but it's still seen as a sport for girls. There's an interesting history to this. By the 1920s, women had begun to play baseball, especially at women's colleges. Several semi-professional "bloomer-girl" barnstorming teams traveled from city to city, and were incredibly popular. In 1943, the All-American Girls Professional Baseball League was established by Phil Wrigley, the man who owned the Chicago Cubs. So many Ameri-

can men were fighting in World War II, baseball players among them, that the rosters of men's baseball teams
were empty. Like the Rosie the Riveter movement that
sent many women to work in factories and gave them

new experiences there, the All-American Girls Professional Baseball League opened up professional baseball to women, all in the name of the war effort, and provided entertainment to the people at home.

Some people never got used to the idea of women playing baseball. They fought against the presence of women in their sport, wanting to keep it the preserve of men and boys. They were successful; the All-American Girls League shut down during the 1950s, and women were shuttled off to play softball instead.

Today, softball is one of only two sports that the National Collegiate Association of Athletics (NCAA) has for women only, the other being field hockey. For four years, from 1976 to 1980, women had a softball league all their own, the International Women's Professional Softball League, but it couldn't compete against the popularity of baseball. Women's softball was played at the Olympics in 1996 for the first time. The United States women's team won the gold medal, and repeated that victory in 2000. It's too bad that in 2012 softball will be dropped from the Olympic roster, along with baseball.

࿐

Greek Columns

Since human beings first moved out of caves, people have looked at their shelter and wondered how to hold the roof up. In an age long before steel beams and concrete, ancient Greek architects dreamed of creating buildings that felt perfect and sublime. To do so, they developed three orders, or systems, of columns. The three column orders were not just directions for decorating a column's capital, shaft, and base, they were a vision for how all the elements of the building—the columns and the roof and the platform—would work together to build harmony, symmetry, and balance.

DORIC

The Doric order is the oldest and simplest. The capital is a circle that is topped by a square. The column shaft is either plain or fluted (fluted shafts have channeled grooves running from top to bottom). A Doric column has no base. It stands directly on the building's platform.

While Doric columns and capitals are the most austere of the three orders, the area above the columns—called the entablature—is an altogether different matter.

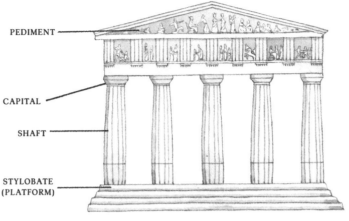

DORIC ORDER

The entablature sits over the columns and below the roof. It has three components. From bottom to top, these are the architrave, the frieze, and the cornice. The first, and lowest, is the architrave, a stone beam that sits right on top of the columns. In the middle of the entablature is the frieze. The frieze is comprised of two alternating elements: the metope (pronounced me-to-pee, with the accent of the first syllable) and the triglyph. The metope is a rectangular space that is decorated with carved sculptures or painted pictures. Next to it is always a triglyph, characterized by its three vertical lines. To add even more

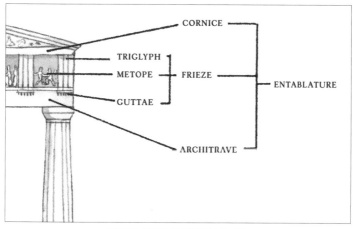

DETAIL VIEW OF ENTABLATURE

visual interest to the building, beneath each triglyph ancient Greek builders placed small guttae ("drops"). This frieze continues on all four sides of the building.

Just above the frieze is the entablature's final and highest element: the cornice. This is a simple marble band, or ledge. Atop the entire entablature is the pediment. This is the triangle formed by the two sloping sides of the roof, and inside this triangle is even more carved sculpture. The pediment is often filled to the brim with sculptures of Greek heroes, heroines, and mythological scenes.

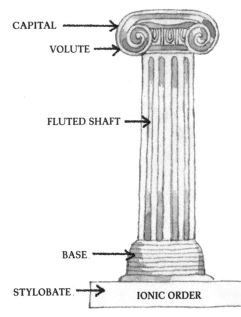

CAPITAL

VOLUTE

FLUTED SHAFT

BASE

STYLOBATE

IONIC ORDER

IONIC

The Ionic order is more stylized. The capital has two scrolls, called volutes. Beneath these are egg-and-dart carvings or other chiseled borders. A marble band separates the capital from the column shaft. Ionic columns have shafts that are taller and more slender than those of the Doric order, and they are usually fluted. The Ionic shaft rests on a base that looks like a stack of rings, and that base rests on the building's platform.

CORINTHIAN

The Corinthian order developed last, and it is the most elaborate. The capital has two small volute scrolls at the very top. The rest of the basket-shaped capital overflows with fancifully carved acanthus leaves, flowers, spirals, and fruit. Corinthian columns have a fluted shaft and a base much like the Ionic order.

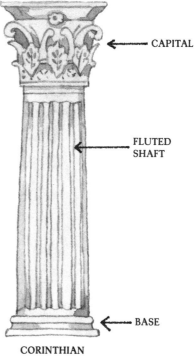

CAPITAL

FLUTED
SHAFT

BASE

CORINTHIAN
ORDER

Fun Fact: In 333 BC, the Greek commander Alexander the Great led his armies across Asia and into India, spreading Greek culture along the way. This capital from India, carved several centuries after Alexander's travels, mixes the Greek Corinthian order with images of the Buddha.

IN AMERICA

In the nineteenth century, United States President Thomas Jefferson became enamored with Greek buildings. He admired their simplicity and grandeur, and felt that they mirrored his ideals for America. Jefferson helped to popularize this Greek Revival style, and that's why so many of our public buildings have Greek column orders. The Second Bank of the United States in Philadelphia was built in Doric style. The United States Capitol has several Corinthian columns with carvings of tobacco leaves and corncobs. The main entrance to the United States Supreme Court has two rows of huge, Corinthian columns, and a slogan etched in the architrave reads "Equal Justice Under the Law."

Public Speaking

If you would rather die than speak in public, you're in good company: glossophobia (fear of speaking in public, or "stage fright") affects as much as 75 percent of the population. But speaking in front of a group doesn't have to be nerve-racking, especially if you practice before you do it. Public speaking shares many of the principles of a good negotiation: Preparation, Practice, and Presenting—with the confidence to "seal the deal."

PREPARE

Know what you're going to say

Write out your speech, and practice saying it aloud. You don't necessarily need to memorize it, but you should know it well enough so that if you had to talk without your notes, you could pull it off.

Know who you're going to say it to

Knowing your audience is good advice no matter what you are performing. If you know you will be giving a speech in your history class, that's going to inform your material much differently than if you were giving a toast at your dad's 50th birthday party. You want to adapt your speech to fit the people you are speaking to. That way nobody gets bored, and what you say will be a good match for your audience.

Know where you're going to say it

It's a good idea to familiarize yourself with the place where you'll be speaking, if you can. Is it a big room or a small one? Will you have to speak loud and project, or will there be a microphone that you will have to adjust? Is there a lectern or a chair, or will you be able to move around while you talk? When you have some information about where you'll be, you'll know what to expect before you get there, and that will help cut down on your nerves once it's showtime.

PRACTICE

Visualize

Most of the fear we have around public speaking isn't about talking in front of people, but about doing something potentially embarrassing in front of people. To combat this, practice imagining yourself giving your speech and doing a great job. Walk yourself through it in your head, from beginning to end, giving yourself a chance to visualize yourself doing well instead of living out your worst fears.

Realize

Make it real by practicing your speech ahead of time—by yourself, in front of your family, in front of your friends, the family pets, whoever you can get to be an audience for you. It's a good idea to either write out your speech on notecards or print it out in a very big font so that you can quickly look down, see what you need to say, and look back up to say it. Practicing delivering your speech so that it becomes routine will stand you in good stead when you start to feel unnerved onstage or in front of the class. Practicing with an audience is also a chance to realize that your audience wants you to succeed. People want to hear what you have to say, and they want you to do well.

Exercise

If you are waiting around while others speak before you, it is helpful to step outside the room just before you speak to calm yourself down with deep-breathing exercises, breathing in slowly through your nose and breathing out through your mouth. If you're too nervous to breathe, you might channel that energy into a quick set of jumping jacks, or shaking out your arms and legs. Then take some deep breaths to feel calm and centered. This is something you can do in practice and in performance.

PRESENT

It's not about you

Remember as you begin your presentation, it's about your speech, not about you. It's helpful to concentrate on the message—not the medium. That way instead of thinking about all the different ways things could go wrong as you deliver your talk, you focus yourself on the content of your talk and about getting those points across.

It's all about you

Whether or not you crumble out of nervousness or do fantastically well thanks to sheer nerve is completely up to you—in other words, it is in your control. When you're incredibly nervous, you have the opportunity to harness that energy and transform it into vitality and enthusiasm. Take a deep breath and dive in!

QUICK TIPS

Keep it short and sweet.

Slow down: Don't talk too fast.

Look up! If it's too scary to look at the audience in the front row, look at the people in the back of the room.

Smile: Look confident, even if you don't feel confident.

Pretend: Pull a "Brady Bunch," where you imagine everyone in the audience is sitting there in their underwear. Find a friendly face in the audience and pretend you're only talking to that person.

Practice: Join the debate team, dare yourself to speak up in class, give a speech in front of a mirror. The more opportunities you have to speak in public, the easier it gets.

Biggest asset: Self-confidence. Act as though you have a right to be there—because you do.

It's all good

No matter how you do, it is always good in the sense that every time you speak in public, you gain experience. Use this to build your sense of self-confidence: if you've done well, you now have proof for the next time around that you can do well. And if nerves have gotten the best of you, you now have proof that the worst has happened and you've survived. Either way, you know that you've done it—you've spoken in public once, and you can do it again. This confidence-building is crucial, because having confidence is the key to speaking well.

∂

Women's Olympic Firsts

❖ In Ancient Greece, women were barred from competing in the Olympics and instead had their own athletic games of Hera every four years. In 1896, at the first modern Olympics in Greece, women were still not allowed to compete. A Greek woman, Stamati Revithi, unofficially ran the marathon and was referred to by the officials as 'Melpomene,' the Greek muse of Tragedy.

❖ The first modern Olympic games to officially include women were the 1900 summer games in Paris, France. Golfer Margaret T. Abbott is the first American woman to win an Olympic gold medal.

❖ Women's boxing is included for the first time in 1904, and only in 1928 does women's gymnastics become an official Olympic sport. 1928 is also the year that women are allowed to compete in track and field events for the first time, and American Elizabeth Robinson becomes the first female gold medalist in a track and field event in Olympic history, winning the 100 meters dash.

- ❖ At the 1932 Summer Games in Los Angeles, California, track stars Louise Stokes and Tydia Pickett become the first black female competitors in the Olympics Games.

- ❖ In 1936, thirteen-year-old diver Marjorie Gestering becomes the youngest Olympic gold medalist ever when she wins the springboard event.

- ❖ At the summer games in 1952, women and men compete together for the first time in Olympic equestrian events. Women gymnasts compete in individual apparatus events for the first time, and Soviet Maria Gorokhovskaya wins the first all-around gold for the USSR in its first Olympics ever. She also is the first woman to win seven medals in a single Olympics.

- ❖ Basketball becomes an Olympic event for women for the first time in 1976. It is at these games that Nadia

Comaneci becomes the first gymnast ever—male or female—to score a perfect 10 in an Olympic event; she is also the youngest Olympic gymnastics all-around champion ever.

❖ In 1984, Candy Costie and Tracie Ruiz win the first gold medal awarded for duet synchronized swimming. Mary Lou Retton becomes the first American woman to win the all-around title for the Olympic gold medal, and the first American to earn a perfect score. Joan Benoit Samuelson wins the first Olympic women's marathon. And Connie Carpenter-Phinney wins the first Olympic gold medal ever awarded for cycling.

❖ At the winter games in Calgary in 1988, figure skater Debi Thomas becomes the first African-American to win an Olympic medal in ice skating.

❖ At the 1992 summer games in Barcelona, Spain, 13-year-old platform diver Fu Mingxia of China becomes the second-youngest person to win an individual gold medal.

❖ Speed skater Bonnie Blair becomes the first American woman to win five gold medals at the 1994 winter games.

❖ At the 2000 summer games in Sydney, Australia, Cathy Freeman becomes the first Aboriginal woman to win an individual Olympic medal.

❖ At the 2002 winter games, short track speedskater Yang Yang becomes the first Chinese athlete, male or female, to win a gold medal. Bobsledder Vonetta becomes the first black athlete to earn winter gold. And ice skater Naomi Lang is the first Native American female athlete to participate in the Olympic winter games.

❖ In 2004, in Athens, Greece, women's wrestling is introduced, with 21 nations qualifying to send wrestlers to the games.

❖ In the 2006 winter games, Claudia Pechstein becomes the first female Winter Olympian to win medals in five consecutive Olympics, and is the most

successful German Winter Olympian of all time.
Tanith Belbin, along with her partner Benjamin
Agosto, wins the silver medal for ice dancing—the
first medal for the U.S. in ice dancing in 30 years.
Tanja Poutiainen earns the first medal in alpine
skiing for Finland when she wins silver in the giant
slalom. And the Swedish team wins women's curling
and become the first curling team to ever hold
Olympic, World, and European titles at the same
time.

Spanish Terms

TERMS OF ENDEARMENT

Mi chula
My pretty one

Querida
Darling

Hermanita
Little sister

Muñeca
Doll

FUN WORDS TO SAY

Chimichanga
(chim-ee-chahng-guh)
A crisp tortilla with a spicy meat filling.

Burro
(boo-row) (be sure to roll the "R"!)
Donkey; stupid (*Como burro* means, "like a donkey").

Tonto
(tahn-toe)
Silly or foolish.

Chistosa
(chee-stoh-sa)
Funny; a facetious attitude.

Parangaricutirimicuaro
(pahr-rahn-gahr-ee-koo-tee-ree-MEE-kwahr-row)
The name of a town in the Southern part of Mexico;
used as a nonsensical tongue-twister in much the same
way as "supercalifragilisticexpialidocious."

EXPRESSIONS

Este arroz ya se coció.
"That rice has been cooked."
(Similar to our expression, "That ship has sailed.")

De tal palo tal astilla.
"Of such a stick is the chip."
(Like our phrase, "A chip off the old block.")

No se puede tapar el sol con un dedo.
"You can't cover the sun with one finger."

Al mejor cocinero, se le queman los frijoles.
"Even the best cook burns his beans."

Porque naces en horno, ¡no quiere decir que eres una barra de pan!
"Just because you were born in an oven doesn't make you a loaf of bread!"

¡El mero, mero patatero!
"The real, real potato seller!"
(Like "The real McCoy," or "It's the real thing!")

Daring Spanish Girls

ARANTXA SANCHEZ-VICARIO

Born in Barcelona, Spain, in 1971, Arantxa Sanchez-Vicario started playing tennis at age four, following in her older brothers' footsteps. When she was 17, she won the French Open, defeating the number-one ranked player in the world, Steffi Graf, and becoming the youngest woman ever to win the singles title. (Her record was broken the next year, when 16-year-old Monica Seles won.) Arantxa gained the nickname "Barcelona Bumblebee" due her tenaciousness and her refusal to surrender points without a fight, even if it meant flying all over the court. She became the world number-one ranked singles player in 1995, competed in the Olympics three times, and over the course of her career won four Grand Slam singles titles and six Grand Slam doubles titles. She was also the first woman since Martina Navrátilová in 1987 to simultaneously hold the number one ranking in both singles and doubles. In 2007, Arantxa was inducted into the International Tennis Hall of Fame—only the third Spanish player (and the first Spanish woman) to achieve such an honor.

CRISTINA SÁNCHEZ DE PABLOS

The bullfighter Cristina Sánchez de Pablos was born in Madrid in 1972 and debuted as a bullfighter in Madrid exactly one week before her twenty-first birthday. She enjoyed tremendous international success as one of the first females in the sport ("matadoras"), performing to great acclaim at bullrings in Mexico and Ecuador as well as Spain. During her career, she earned a total of 316 cuts. She retired in 1999.

ELENA GOMEZ SERVERA

Elena Gomez Servera, born November 14, 1985, on the island of Mallorca, Spain, was the first Spanish gymnast ever to win a World Championship title, and the first gymnast ever to complete a quadruple turn in competition. She won the World Championship title in 2002, and in 2003 she won the World Cup competition in Paris on the floor exercise and the bronze medal at the Anaheim World Championships. At the 2004 Olympics in Athens, Elena reached the finals on two events and finished in eighth place in the All-Around, helping the Spanish team achieve fifth-place standing. In 2006, Elena retired from competition after suffering a back injury.

૱

Boys

Without a doubt you have already received many confusing messages about what, if anything, you should be doing with boys. Some girls are led to believe that being liked by boys is important above all else. Some girls are told that boys are different, and that girls should adapt themselves to be like the boys they like or take care not to be too threatening—learn about sports if a boy likes sports, or pretend to be stupid about subjects a boy likes to excel in. Some girls are encouraged to think of boys as protectors, or, alternately, as creatures that need protecting. It may seem to some girls that suddenly boys matter a whole lot more than they should; still others wonder what all the fuss is about.

Many things are said of boys: Boys like sports, boys are messy, boys don't have any feelings, boys like trucks, boys don't like girly things, boys like to run around and eat gross food. Whatever the specific generalization, the point of these notions about boys is to set them apart from girls as being entirely different.

Similar statements are made about girls: Girls like pink, girls like flowers, girls are neat and clean, girls are frivolous, girls are emotional. Are any of these things true about all girls? Of course not. But it's easier to think about boys and girls as being entirely different than it is to think about boys and girls as having lots of common ground.

As concerns boys themselves, you have several options. The first, of course, is to ignore them until you (and they) are 19. Or 21. Or 25.

Alternately, you could make a boy your best friend. Boys can be excellent friends. In general, they like to do things, and that makes them rather fun.

Of course a third option is romance. Some girls might be interested in this kind of thing (you will recognize them by their doodles of their name and a boy's name in a heart on their science homework); other girls might think that would be too icky to even imagine. If you are in the latter group, don't worry, you have plenty of company.

If you are in the former group, there are two main things to keep in mind. One, if a boy doesn't like you the way you are, the problem is him, not you. And two, don't try to make a boy change for you—it's important to appreciate people for who they are.

Wherever you fall on the spectrum of how you feel about boys, do treat all your friends, boys and girls, with kindness. This has gone out of fashion, and that's a sad mistake.

Overall, the truth is that there's no great big mystery about boys. Boys are people, and like all people, they are complicated. And that's what makes being friends with other people interesting: you get to learn about how other people think and act, and, in the process, learn a little bit more about yourself.

∾

Princesses Today

When most of us think of princesses, we conjure up fairy tales and Disney movies, lovely Cinderella or Belle in their pale blue taffeta and yellow silk ball gowns—or the ultra-pink princess merchandise pushed on girls today.

Perhaps it's a surprise to find beneath the glitter that these are real people who are princesses, and who lead very different lives than we see in the sugary movies— princesses who are comfortable wearing sensible wool suits and athletic clothes more often than fancy dresses and sparkly jewels.

Thirty-nine nations in the world still have monarchies—constitutional monarchies, which means the royal family is important, but that the real political power is in the elected parliament and the Prime Minister. Many of these monarchies include princesses, of all ages— some born into their royal family, like princesses Kako and Aiko of Japan, and some married in, like commoner Princess Mette-Marit of Norway.

However they became princesses, these real girls and women are as different from one another as any girls can be. Many do live with great wealth and privilege, true, but their lives can be quite conventional. They go to school, start businesses (like Princess Naa Asie Ocansey of Ghana, who has had a TV home-shopping show), and do charity work. Some are happy with their lives, and others struggle with their royal role, as did the late Diana, Princess of Wales, and the late Princess Leila of Iran.

Real princesses have various personalities, talents, and hobbies. Princess Maha Chakri Sirindhorn of Thailand writes poetry and short stories, plays Thai classical instruments, and also jogs, swims, bikes, and treks.

A closer look at modern-day princesses gives you an idea of the many ways to live a real life of royalty today—and not one of these princesses resembles Sleeping Beauty.

An Equestrian Princess

Her Royal Highness Haya bint Al Hussein—also known as Princess Haya—was born in 1974 and grew up in the royal family of Jordan. Her father is the late King Hussein, and her mother is Queen Alia Al Hussein. She attended St. Hilda's College in Oxford, England, studying politics, philosophy, and economics. She is an avid sportswoman who competes in equestrian sports (horse competitions being a popular royal pastime), including the 2000 Summer Olympics at Sydney.

In 2004, when she was thirty, Princess Haya married His Highness Sheik Muhammed, the Prime Minister and Ruler of Dubai, and moved to that vibrant city in the United Arab Emirates to be with him. In her role as princess, Haya leads many humanitarian efforts. She advocates for children's right to play and for health care, and served as the first woman ambassador to the United Nations hunger relief program.

An Everygirl Princess

Mary Elizabeth Donaldson fits the image of the ordinary girl who becomes a royal princess. Born in Australia in 1972, she grew up on the island of Tasmania, where her father was a math professor. She played field hockey and swam, and after graduation from college, she worked for an ad agency and in public relations.

She met her future husband, Crown Prince Frederik of Denmark, at a pub in Sydney; he was in town for the 2000 Olympics. In 2004 they had a grand wedding—800 guests at the Copenhagen Cathedral—and Mary Elizabeth became the new princess of Denmark. They have since had two children: Prince Christian, born in 2005, and Princess Isabella, born in April 2007.

A Champion Fighter Princess

Her Highness Sheikha Maitha bint Muhammed al-Maktum has not traveled the standard princess-and-horses route. Born in 1980 to Sheik Muhammed bin Rashid Al Maktum of Dubai and the United Arab Emirates, Maitha has followed her passion for the martial arts and is a karate champion.

Princess Maitha has won gold medals at Tae Kwon Do championships, competes in international karate championships, and was named the Arab world's best female athlete.

An Unassuming Princess

Most people know that Prince Charles is the eldest son of Queen Elizabeth, the reigning Queen of England, and know of Charles' famous late wife, Diana. However, not as many people talk of Charles' only sister, Anne—which is just how she wants it. Anne was born in 1950, and her full title is HRH The Princess Anne Elizabeth, Princess Royal, which denotes that she is the eldest daughter of the Queen.

Although she has not abdicated her royal status, she has led a very unassuming life outside the public eye. When she married, her first husband declined to take a royal title, even though it is considered common to do so. She chose not to pass on royal titles to her children, Peter and Zara, in order to protect them from the spotlight that hovers over children in the British royal family.

A Young Lady Princess

The youngest girl of the British royal line has also side-stepped the title Princess. Born in 2003 to Prince Edward (Charles' younger brother) and his wife Sophie, who are also known as the Earl and Countess of Wessex, little Louise was given the title Lady instead.

The princess title is still legally hers, and when she comes of age, she can fully adopt it if she wishes.

A Rediscovered Princess

And here's one final princess story, that of Sarah Culberson, born in 1976. Her mother and father met in college in West Virginia, fell in love, and had Sarah, but they put her up for adoption just two days after she was born. When she was twenty-two and living in San Francisco, Sarah hired an investigator to find her birth parents. She learned that her mother, a native West Virginian,

Sarah Culberson

had died of cancer many years before, but that her father was a royal member of the Mende Tribe in Bumpe, Sierra Leone. He was of the line of Paramount Chief, and as his long-lost daughter, Sarah was officially a princess.

Now that she has claimed her title, Sarah's life as a princess isn't about horses and galas. Sierra Leone had a devastatingly long civil war, and much of her family's village, including the school, is in shambles. Sarah has focused her efforts on raising money in the United States to send back to her tribe so they can rebuild their village and school.

Queens Of the Ancient World: Zenobia

In the third century AD, Zenobia of Palmyra was the famed Queen of the East. According to the author of Historia Augusta, she had long black hair and warm brown skin, piercing dark eyes and a lyrical, strong voice. Known for her boldness, determination, and fairness as a leader, she was just in her twenties when she built and ruled an empire that covered most of what is now the Middle East.

Zenobia was born around 240 AD at Palmyra, a sparkling, palm-tree-filled paradise deep in the desert of Syria (now the ruins of Tadmor, about 150 miles northeast of Damascus). Her father was a tribal ruler who had enticed her mother from Egypt to this prosperous and cosmopolitan trading outpost.

Zenobia's full given name was Iulia Aurelia Zenobia. "Iulia" was a popular girl's name in Rome, which, even though it was far away, ruled the Syrian desert. "Aurelia" meant that her family were Roman citizens, an important honor. "Zenobia" came from her family's Aramaic tribe. Historians know that by the age of eighteen,

she had already married the governor of Palmyra, a man named Odainat (known in Latin as Septimius Odaenathus). Then she changed her name to Septimia Zenobia, to match his.

As wife to the land's governor, Zenobia was well educated, and her court was filled with philosophers and poets. Many an evening was spent lingering over sumptuous meals, talking about Homer and Plato, making speeches, and laughing at riddles and wit. The peace was disturbed in 260, however, when the Persian king, Shapur, tried to take Syria from the Romans. As allies of Rome, the Palmyrans guarded the frontier where the

Roman Empire met the Persian, so Odainat and Zenobia prepared for combat.

The emperor of Rome, Valerian, faced rebellion everywhere—to the west, north, and now to the east. His troops were dispirited, but nonetheless he marched them to battle. The Persians had superior strength and fighting skills, so they easily routed the weary Roman soldiers. Valerian and Shapur agreed to meet at the city of Edessa and negotiate terms. When Valerian showed up, the Persians ambushed him and took him into captivity.

That's when two Roman messengers urged their horses across the desert sand to Palmyra, bringing the terrible news of Valerian's capture. Odainat and Zenobia were ready. Side by side, the couple donned armor, saddled their horses, and led the army of Palmyra against the Persians, in search of Valerian.

While Odainat was a courageous and daring warrior, ancient writers tell us Zenobia was even more so, and praised her battle skills, including her exceptional way with the troops. She rallied them, kept them inspired, and at times even handed off her horse to march for miles with the foot soldiers. Unfortunately, the Persians killed Valerian before Odainat and Zenobia could save him, but the couple's brave leadership earned them the complete respect of the Palmyran army and people.

Was it odd for these troops to see a woman in front, her long black hair streaming out from beneath her helmet? The ancient cultures of Greece and Rome often portrayed the deity of war as a woman, and female Victory statues graced nearly every city. In fact, the Palmyran soldiers followed Zenobia to battle again and again in the following years.

In 267 AD, seven years after their first battle together, Zenobia's husband Odainat was assassinated. The royal line fell to Zenobia's toddler son, Vaballathus, who was clearly too young to rule. Zenobia, then 27 years old, became queen in his stead. She dreamed of an empire of Palmyra and prepared the troops for a battle of independence.

The Romans were busy in Europe defending themselves from the Goths, Zenobia knew, so she attacked the Roman province of Egypt. The Egyptians, too, were distracted, off battling pirates in the Mediterranean Sea. She conquered them, and then went to conquer cities in Arabia, Palestine, and Syria. By 269, she declared her empire's independence from Rome and minted new coins with her image and the word "REGINA"—Queen.

Historians tell us that Zenobia ruled tolerantly as Queen of the East, drawing on the Palmyran traditions of hospitality and openness to treat all people with fairness, including the pagans, Jews, and Christians of her empire. She opened new trade routes and met with Christian bishops and other leaders of the cities she conquered.

As Zenobia grew her Palmyran empire, armies threatened the larger Roman Empire on all sides. The new Roman emperor, Aurelian, was battling the Goth and Visigoth tribes in northern Europe. When his messengers arrived with news of Queen Zenobia's expanding kingdom, Aurelian set off for Egypt, determined to win the territory back, and then to Turkey (which in ancient times was called Asia Minor). After these small victories, he prepared to attack Antioch, a city in northern Syria that Zenobia now ruled.

Zenobia had never faced the vast legions of the mighty Roman army. She could have given up and returned to the Roman fold, but decided instead to take a last stand and save the heart of her hard-earned empire. She assembled the troops along one side of the north-flowing Orontes River. Her soldiers fought all day, Zenobia along with them. Then, as the sun dipped toward the western horizon, the tired soldiers, bleary and water-starved after a long day, fell into a trap, in which the Romans massacred them from all sides.

Zenobia managed to escape with seventy thousand soldiers and retreated to the city of Emesa. They found a hill and, under cover of night, climbed to the top and lay in wait, ready to rain down arrows on the Roman soldiers. The Romans, though, pulled out their colorful shields, held high overhead, each shield meeting the next to cover the men and protect them from the Palmyrans' arrows and darts. In this formation, the Romans pushed forward up the hill. When they reached the Palmyran marksmen, they moved their shields forward and down, and attacked.

Thousands of troops died on the battlefield. Zenobia herself barely escaped and even her trusted horse fell in the battle. She commandeered a camel and turned the slow beast toward the sandy hinterlands of the Syrian desert, with hopes that the plodding animal could take her one hundred miles east to Persia, where she would be safe from Rome.

"I promise you life if you surrender," Aurelian wrote

to her. Zenobia had other plans, but it was Aurelian's turn for victory. He lay siege to her beloved Palmyra and sent his best soldiers on horseback to capture the fallen paradise's fugitive queen. As she neared the Euphrates River, so close to freedom, the emperor's horsemen reached Zenobia and captured her.

The remainder of Zenobia's life is shrouded in myth. Where one ancient historian reports that she died in captivity, another writes that Aurelian took her to Rome. It is said that in 274, Zenobia was wrapped in chains of gold and made to walk down Rome's main boulevard as Aurelian celebrated his triumph over the many tribes he had battled. Still another tale suggests that some time later, Zenobia was released. In her absence, Palmyra had rebelled against Rome once more and had been crushed. Some tales hold that with no home to return to, Zenobia lived the rest of her life not far from Rome, in Tivoli.

What Is the Bill of Rights?

In the days after the United States won its independence from Britain in the 1780s, people vigorously debated how much power a government needed to rule, and how best to protect people's rights from being overly stifled by the government. The now-famous Federalist and Anti-Federalist papers were originally published as letters in newspapers, and instead of using their given names, the letter writers often took names like "Brutus," "Agrippa," and "Cato"—well-known figures from the era of the Roman Republic. In their struggle to create a free society, after having only known life under a king, the early Americans looked to ancient Roman society for inspiration.

The first ten amendments to the Constitution, called the Bill of Rights, were the answer to the power of gov-

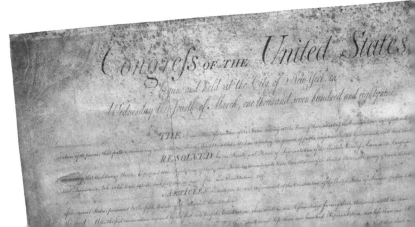

ernment versus personal freedom debate. The amendments form our basic sense of what it means to be American. These are the laws that now protect our freedom of religion and speech, our independent press, and our right to assemble peacefully in protest. Among other things, the Bill of Rights establishes our right to bear arms (not arm bears) and to be granted fair and speedy trials, and protects us from cruel and unusual punishment.

THE PREAMBLE TO THE BILL OF RIGHTS

Congress of the United States begun and held at the City of New-York, on Wednesday the fourth of March, one thousand seven hundred and eighty nine.

The Conventions of a number of the States having, at the time of adopting the Constitution, expressed a desire, in order to prevent misconstruction or abuse of its powers, that further declaratory and restrictive clauses should be added, and as extending the ground of public confidence in the Government will best insure the beneficent ends of its institution;

Resolved, by the Senate and House of Representatives of the United States of America, in Congress assembled, two-thirds of both Houses concurring, that the following articles be proposed to the Legislatures of the several States, as amendments to the Constitution of the United States; all or any of which articles, when ratified by three-fourths of the said Legislatures, to be valid to all intents and purposes as part of the said Constitution, namely: Ratified December 15, 1791

AMENDMENT I

Congress shall make no law respecting an establishment of religion, or prohibiting the free exercise thereof; or abridging the freedom of speech, or of the press; or the right of the people peaceably to assemble, and to petition the government for a redress of grievances.

AMENDMENT II

A well regulated militia, being necessary to the security of a free state, the right of the people to keep and bear arms, shall not be infringed.

AMENDMENT III

No soldier shall, in time of peace be quartered in any house, without the consent of the owner, nor in time of war, but in a manner to be prescribed by law.

AMENDMENT IV

The right of the people to be secure in their persons, houses, papers, and effects, against unreasonable searches and seizures, shall not be violated, and no warrants shall issue, but upon probable cause, supported by oath or affirmation, and particularly describing the place to be searched, and the persons or things to be seized.

AMENDMENT V

No person shall be held to answer for a capital, or otherwise infamous crime, unless on a presentment or indictment of a grand jury, except in cases arising in the land or naval forces, or in the militia, when in actual service in time of war or public danger; nor shall any person be subject for the same offense to be twice put in jeopardy of life or limb; nor shall be compelled in any criminal case to be a witness against himself, nor be deprived of life, liberty, or property, without due process of law; nor shall private property be taken for public use, without just compensation.

AMENDMENT VI

In all criminal prosecutions, the accused shall enjoy the right to a speedy and public trial, by an impartial jury of the state and district wherein the crime shall have been committed, which district shall have been previously ascertained by law, and to be informed of the nature and cause of the accusation; to be confronted with the witnesses against him; to have compulsory process for obtaining witnesses in his favor, and to have the assistance of counsel for his defense.

AMENDMENT VII

In suits at common law, where the value in controversy shall exceed twenty dollars, the right of trial by jury shall be preserved, and no fact tried by a jury, shall be otherwise reexamined in any court of the United States, than according to the rules of the common law.

AMENDMENT VIII

Excessive bail shall not be required, nor excessive fines imposed, nor cruel and unusual punishments inflicted.

AMENDMENT IX

The enumeration in the Constitution, of certain rights, shall not be construed to deny or disparage others retained by the people.

AMENDMENT X

The powers not delegated to the United States by the Constitution, nor prohibited by it to the states, are reserved to the states respectively, or to the people.

Seventeen amendments follow these. The last, ratified in 1992, made it harder for our Senators and Representatives to raise their own salaries. This amendment has a long and intriguing history; it was first submitted in 1779 as part of a heated debate about states rights! Amendments are first passed by a two-thirds majority of the full Congress—the Senate and the House of Representatives. Then they must be approved, or ratified, by the legislatures of seventy-five percent of the states. This often means years of spirited discussion for each attempt to pass a new amendment.

The history of the amendments highlights our nation's most impassioned debates. In 1868, the thirteenth amendment abolished slavery. Two years later, the fifteenth guaranteed that our right to vote could not be denied on account of our race, color, or having previously been a slave. The eighteenth amendment made it illegal to manufacture alcohol—and ushered in the prohibition years (which ended two years later, when the amendment was repealed).

In 1920, the nineteenth amendment marked a significant event for girls and women in America when, after 141 years of male-only elections, women were granted the right to vote. Just afterward, Alice Paul, one of the suffragettes, or activists on behalf of women's voting, or suffrage, presented to Congress an amendment to supply equal rights to women. It wasn't until the 1970s, however, that both houses of Congress sent this amendment to the states to ratify. Although the Equal Rights Amendment came close to approval by thirty-eight of our fifty states, the necessary three-quarters, it was defeated.

Books That Will Change Your Life

We present these titles for your reading pleasure, knowing there are endless books beyond this list to discover and love, too. We know you will read them in your own fashion and at your own pace.

20 GIRL CLASSICS

- *A Wrinkle in Time* by Madeleine L'Engle, and her other books too.
- *Anne of Green Gables* (and *Emily of New Moon*) by L.M. Montgomery
- *Behind Rebel Lines: The Incredible Story of Emma Edmonds, Civil War Spy* by Seymour Reit
- *Bridge to Terabithia* by Katherine Paterson
- *Caddie Woodlawn* (and the sequel, *Magical Melons*) by Carol Ryrie Brink
- *Charlotte's Web* by E.B.White
- *The Famous Five,* a series by Enid Blyton, with Dick, Ann, Julian, George (a girl!), and her dog Timothy.
- *From the Mixed-Up Files of Mrs. Basil E. Frankweiler* by E.L. Konigsburg

- *Harriet the Spy* by Louise Fitzhugh
- *The Illyrian Adventure* series by Lloyd Alexander
- *The Little Princess* (and *The Secret Garden)* by Frances Hodgson Burnett
- *Keep Climbing, Girls* by Beah H. Richards
- *Little Women* and *Jo's Boys* by Louisa May Alcott
- *Little House on the Prairie* by Laura Ingalls Wilder —the entire series.
- *Lizzie Bright (*and *The Buckminster Boy)* by Gary Schmidt
- *Mandy* by Julie Andrews
- *Matilda* (and *The BFG)* by Roald Dahl. Actually, make that anything by Roald Dahl.
- *Miss Happiness and Miss Flower* by Rumer Godden
- *Pippi Longstocking* by Astrid Lindgren
- *Ramona* by Beverly Cleary (the series)

OTHER FAVORITES

- *Alice's Adventures in Wonderland* and *Through the Looking Glass* by Lewis Carroll
- *Amazing Grace* by Mary Hoffman
- *All of a Kind Family* by Sydney Taylor

- *The Borrowers* by Mary Norton
- *Call of the Wild* by Jack London
- *The Chronicles of Narnia* by C.S. Lewis. Seven classic novels from the 1950s, including the most famous, *The Lion, the Witch, and the Wardrobe*
- *The Good Earth* by Pearl S. Buck
- *Great Expectations* by Charles Dickens
- *Harry Potter* by J.K. Rowling. All seven, in time, and as you grow.
- *The Hobbit* and *The Lord of the Rings* by J.R.R. Tolkien
- *The Hoboken Chicken Emergency* and other madcap stories by Daniel Pinkwater
- *Island of the Blue Dolphins,* by Scott O'Dell, about a girl Robinson Crusoe. When you're done, read the original *Robinson Crusoe* by Daniel Defoe.
- *Jane Eyre* by Charlotte Brontë
- *Johnny Tremain* by Esther Forbes
- *The Little Prince* by Antoine de Saint-Exupery
- *Marjorie Morningstar* by Herman Wouk
- *Mary Poppins* by P.L. Travers
- *Mrs. Frisby and the Rats of NIMH,* by Robert C. O'Brien

- *My Side of the Mountain* and *Julie of the Wolves* by Jean Craighead George
- *Out of the Dust* by Karen Hesse
- *The Phantom Tollbooth* by Norton Juster. Yes, another boy-hero-rescues-the-princesses plot (though here the princesses are Rhyme and Reason), but a great book nonetheless.
- *Pride and Prejudice* by Jane Austen
- *Treasure Island* by Robert Louis Stevenson
- *A Tree Groes in Brooklyn* by Betty Smith
- *The True Confessions of Charlotte Doyle* by Avi
- *Winnie the Pooh* by A.A. Milne. The original books, and the poems.
- *The Witch of Blackbird Pond* by Elizabeth George Speare
- *Wuthering Heights* by Emily Brontë
- *The Wonderful Wizard of Oz* by Frank Baum

SCIENCE FICTION AND FANTASY BOOKS

- Lloyd Alexander's *The Chronicles of Prydain*
- Isaac Asimov's *Foundation* and *Robot* series
- Ray Bradbury's *Dandelion Wine* and *Fahrenheit 451*
- Orson Scott Card's *Ender's Game* and all the books

in the Ender series
- Susan Cooper's *The Dark is Rising* sequence
- Lois Lowry's *The Giver, Gathering Blue,* and *Messenger*
- Ursula K. LeGuin's *The Tombs of Atuan* and her *Earthsea* trilogy
- Anne McCaffrey's *Dragonsong* trilogy
- Robin McKinley's *The Blue Sword* and *The Hero and the Crown*
- Philip Pullman's *His Dark Materials*

NONFICTION

When we were young and bored, our parents told us, "Go read the dictionary!" We did, and look where it got us. One should never underestimate the pleasure to be found flipping through a dictionary, an encyclopedia, or an old science book.

☙

First Aid

First Aid is basic care in the event of illness, accident, or injury that can be performed by anyone until professional medical treatment is given. It was a concept put first put into practice by the Knights Hospitaller, who came up with the term "first aid" and founded the Order of St. John in the 11th century to train knights in the treatment of common battlefield injuries. In a life of adventure, accidents are bound to happen, and a daring girl needs to know about first aid—even if she never plans to be injured in battle.

The information below is not intended to be a substitute for professional medical advice or treatment. Taking a first aid class will provide even more in-depth instruction. But there are definitely actions you can take to help in the event of injury, and below are some tips and techniques to keep in mind.

REMEMBER YOUR ABCs

When accidents happen, sometimes the first casualty is plain old common sense. It's easy to panic and forget about what's important, but these mnemonics can help you remember what to do. Mnemonic devices are formulas, usually in the form of rhymes, phrases, or acronyms, to help you remember things. Some of the most familiar mnemonics in first aid are the three Ps and the three Bs; the ABCs and CPR; and RICE.

THE THREE Ps

(Preserve life; Prevent further injury; Promote recovery)
Remembering the Three Ps helps you keep in mind what your goal is in responding to an accident or injury: making sure the person stays alive, ensuring that nothing is done to further injure the person, and taking action to help the person recover or get better.

THE THREE Bs

(Breathing; Bleeding; Bones)
The Three Bs remind a first-aid responder of what is most important to check when a person is injured, and the order of importance in treating: Is the person breathing? Is the person bleeding? Are there any broken bones?

ABCs

The ABCs stand for Airway, Breathing, and Circulation, and remembering this helps remind you to check that an injured person has a clear airway passage (isn't choking), is able to breathe, and has a pulse. Open the airway by lifting the person's chin with your fingers, gently tilting their head back. Listen for breathing sounds, look for a rise and fall of the chest, and feel for breathing movement. Check for a pulse by placing two fingers on the person's neck between the voicebox and the muscle on the side of the neck. If a person is not breathing and does not have a pulse, call 911 and begin CPR.

CPR

CPR stands for cardiopulmonary resuscitation, a procedure performed on people whose hearts or breathing has stopped. CPR usually involves two elements: Chest compressions (pressing down on the chest) and rescue breathing (breathing mouth-to-mouth). However, the latest advice from the American Heart Association is that if you are not trained in CPR (meaning you have not taken an accredited first aid training course), you should focus on performing chest compressions only, two per second, until help arrives. This is called "Hands Only" CPR and has two basic steps: Call 911, and compress the chest.

To begin CPR on an adult, make sure the person is on their back, then place your hands one on top of the other on the lower half of the chest, between the nipples. Press straight down using your upper body weight to give two compressions per second. After 30 compressions, re-check pulse and breathing. If necessary, continue performing compressions, checking for progress every 30 compressions, until help arrives. (If you are trained in CPR and rescue breathing, you can perform two rescue breaths at these 30-compression intervals by tilting the person's head back, lifting the chin, pinching the person's nose shut, and breathing directly into the mouth for one second.)

When performing CPR on a child, you should use one hand instead of two to perform chest compressions, but otherwise the procedure is the same. When performing CPR on an infant, use two fingers instead of your whole hand, and compress on the breastbone, just below the nipple line. Give two compressions per second, and check for pulse and breathing after 30 compressions. (If rescue breathing is necessary, tip the baby's head back carefully lifting from the chin, cover the baby's mouth and nose with your mouth, and breathe gently, blowing with your cheeks instead of your lungs, into the baby's mouth. Perform a second rescue breath, then if the baby is still unresponsive, continue performing compressions.)

RICE

Use RICE (Rest, Ice, Compression, and Elevation) for acute injuries like a sprained ankle or injuries due to overuse, like muscle strain.

R (REST): Rest the injured area until pain and swelling go away (usually one to three days).

I (ICE): Within 15 minutes of an injury, apply ice by placing a damp towel over the injured area and putting a cold pack, bag of ice, or a bag of frozen vegetables on top of that. Leave the ice on for 10-30 minutes, then take it off for 30-45 minutes. Repeat this ice on/ice off alteration as often as possible for the next one to three days.

C (COMPRESSION): Use a bandage to apply gentle but firm pressure until the swelling goes down. Beginning a few inches below the injured area, wrap the bandage in an upward spiral; if using compression in addition to ice, wrap the bandage over the ice pack.

E (ELEVATION): Try to keep the injured area above heart level to drain excess fluid.

FOR BURNS, CUTS, AND SCRAPES

Burns are classified by degree. First-degree burns are a reddening of the skin, as in a mild sunburn. Second-degree burns are when the skin blisters. Third-degree burns are when the skin is charred. Treatment for first- and second-degree burns is to immerse in cold water for 15 minutes then apply sterile dressing. For a third-degree burn, cover the burn with a sterile dressing and treat for shock (calm and reassure the injured person, help her maintain a comfortable body temperature with a blanket or by removing her from wind or sun, and have her lay down and elevate her legs 8 to 10 inches). NEVER apply ice, butter, oil, or other substances to a burn.

For cuts and scrapes, rinse the area with cool water. Apply firm but gentle pressure, using gauze, to stop bleeding. If blood soaks through, add more gauze, keeping the first layer in place. Continue to apply pressure.

FOR CHOKING

The universal choking symbol is made by putting your hands around your throat. If you are choking and cannot talk, make this symbol to alert the people around you. If someone who is choking can still talk or is coughing, encourage her to cough more to expel the object. If she cannot talk, or if the cough is weak or ineffective, the Red Cross recommends "Five and Five": Five back blows followed by the five upward thrusts of the Heimlich Maneuver.

Perform five back blows by using the heel of your hand to hit the spot just between a person's shoulder blades. Then do the Heimlich Maneuver: Stand slightly behind the choking person and place your arms around her waist, below her ribcage. Make a fist with one hand, placing your thumb just above her belly button, and grab that fist with your other hand. Give five strong upward-thrusting squeezes to try to lift the diaphragm, forcing air from the lungs and provoking a cough. The cough should move and expel whatever is blocking the airway. Alternate between the five back blows and the five thrusts of the Heimlich Maneuver until the blockage is dislodged. If choking persists, call 911.

If you are alone and choking, it is possible to perform the Heimlich Maneuver on yourself. Place your fist just above your belly button, grab your fist with your other hand, and bend forward over a hard surface like a chair or countertop to help move your fists sharply in and up five times.

EMERGENCIES

Any practiced explorer can tell you that in an emergency, what helps most is being prepared. Make a list of important phone numbers and put them on the wall next to your kitchen phone, or on a notepad stuck to the refrigerator. That way, in the event of an accident, you'll easily find the numbers to call your family doctor, poison control, the fire department, or the police.

The most important emergency number to know, of course, is 911. Calling 911 is free from any phone, even a pay phone. It can be scary to call 911, especially if you're not sure whether or not what you're dealing with is a real emergency, but it's the right thing to do when someone is dangerously hurt, not breathing, or unresponsive. A good rule to remember is when in doubt, make the call.

FIRST AID KIT

It's always a good idea to keep a first aid kit at home, and making one for your family can be a fun project. For the kit itself, you can use a tote bag, backpack, or other container that is clean, roomy, easy to carry, and easy to open.

You can make a mini-kit (with Band-Aids, antibiotic ointment, tweezers, and Ace bandages) to take with you on a hike or when you babysit.

The American College of Emergency Physicians recommends including the following in your first aid kit:

- ✚ Band-Aids of assorted sizes
- ✚ Ace bandages
- ✚ Bandage closures and safety pins
  - Gauze and adhesive tape
  - Sharp scissors with rounded tips
  - Antiseptic wipes
- ✚ Antibiotic ointment
  - Hydrogen peroxide
  - Instant-activating cold packs
- ✚ Tweezers
- ✚ Oral medicine syringe (for children)
  - Prescription medication
- ✚ Medicines including aspirin, ibuprofen, acetaminophen, cough suppressants, antihistamine, decongestants
  - A page listing the contents of your kit for easy reference, your list of emergency phone numbers, and a list of family members' allergies and medications.

IMAGE CREDITS

ALSO AVAILABLE

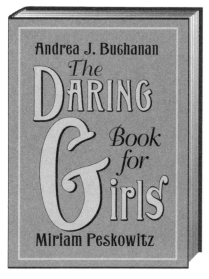

ISBN 978-0-06-147257-2 (hardcover)

Inside You Will Find:

- How to Tie a Sari
- Olympic Female Athletes
- Hopscotch
- Building a Campfire
- Cootie Catchers
- Books That Will Change Your Life
- And much more!

*F*or every girl with an independent spirit and a nose for trouble, here is the original no-boys-allowed guide to everything from camping out to schoolyard games, to great women in history to the rules of Truth or Dare!